This book addresses one of the most important issues for a modern corporation, not just in resources but in any industry. Starting with some really valuable techniques for mapping stakeholders, Witold Henisz goes on to demonstrate with many examples how this data can be integrated and applied. He concludes with very valuable examples of traps to avoid. An excellent guide, whether a company is starting afresh or checking well-developed approaches for potential flaws.

Sir Mark Moody-Stuart, Chairman, Global Compact Foundation; MD, Royal Dutch Shell 1991–2001; author, *Responsible Leadership*

By elevating the importance of corporate diplomacy in creating value and providing a cogent framework to follow, Witold Henisz's work offers a novel analytical rubric that practitioners in all sectors will benefit from.

Ian Bremmer, President & Founder, Eurasia Group; author, *Every Nation for Itself: Winners and Losers in a G-Zero World* **and** *The End of the Free Market: Who Wins the War Between States and Corporations?*

Witold Henisz uses creative rigour to build an important bridge between practitioners of corporate diplomacy and those who may not always value its contribution to business success.

Robert Court, Global Head of External Affairs, Rio Tinto

With trust in corporations at all-time lows and the importance of business and society issues at all time highs, *Corporate Diplomacy* shows how systematic but practical engagement with stakeholders can address both problems.

Ben W. Heineman, Jr, senior fellow at Harvard's schools of law and government; former GE SVP for Law and Public Affairs

Witold Heinsz offers an new paradigm for looking at the increasingly tough political and social challenges which companies face in emerging markets. If your company is facing a blockage or seeking a "license to operate," *Corporate Diplomacy* should be required reading.
Steven Fox, Managing Partner & Founder, Veracity Worldwide LLC

In today's world, more than ever before, the license to operate for any business depends on establishing and maintaining good relationships with the full range of the company's stakeholders. Witold Henisz shows why that matters, the price of not managing it effectively and a clear framework for how to go about it. *Corporate Diplomacy* offers a valuable route map to help business leaders find their path through what can be challenging and unfamiliar terrain.
Lucy Parker and Jon Miller, authors, *Everybody's Business: The Unlikely Story of How Big Business Can Fix the World*

Incisive and thought-provoking. The author tells us the why and how of building stakeholder relations that add value and reduce risk. This book can sharpen the skills that corporations need most in difficult places.
Cameron Hume, Former US Ambassador to Indonesia, Algeria & South Africa; Consultant to Sinar Mas Group

Today's diplomats are found in corporations, the globe-hopping, resource- and talent-rich organizations on the front line of complex issues from human rights to adjudication of water rights. Success as a corporate diplomat requires a remarkable set of talents and skills - from data analysis to deep listening. Professor Henisz's new book is the ultimate field guide to this new brand of diplomacy.
Judith Samuelson, Executive Director, Aspen Institute's Business + Society Program

Call them corporate diplomats, corporate idealists, or government or community relations professionals: Witold Henisz knows that they determine whether global companies fail or succeed. In *Corporate Diplomacy* he speaks directly to them, presenting cases, data, tools, and advice to help them improve outcomes for their companies, affected stakeholders – and consequently the world at large.
Christine Bader, author, *The Evolution of a Corporate Idealist: When Girl Meets Oil*

Witold Henisz's book will define the field of Corporate Diplomacy for the foreseeable future. He illustrates why modern international companies need to invest in this previously unheralded aspect of the leadership craft; and he advances both the science and the art of this critical function. He shows that in the era of big data and analysis, companies can do a lot more to understand and shape the global environment for their products and services, and thus to create value for their own stakeholders. He shows that enlightened companies will place quite as much importance on diplomacy as do governments.
Nick Lovegrove, Senior Director, Albright Stonebridge Group; former Senior Director, McKinsey & Company; former senior advisor, UK Prime Minister's Strategy Unit

Some of the most difficult issues facing extractive industry companies today are *not technical* – they're *human* challenges. Henisz's *Corporate Diplomacy* is a must-read, not just for Community relations or Communications Managers, but for virtually any executive with a decision-making power that inevitably affects external stakeholders. General Managers, CFOs, Human Resources and Procurement professionals, to name a few, need to be the day-to-day corporate diplomats whose actions make or break relationships with stakeholders. This book offers the most insightful, practical thought leadership guidance in the ever-changing field of stakeholder engagement for them to be successful.
Thibaut Millet, Associate Partner, Climate Change & Sustainability, EY

As a practitioner working in the area of stakeholder engagement, *Corporate Diplomacy* provides outstanding guidance on creating an effective stakeholder engagement strategy as well as providing the accompanying practical tools and frameworks to implement it. Witold Henisz illustrates the ever-present dynamic in the corporate environment, that it is essential to show both your external and internal stakeholders that your work is supported by sound strategy as well as clear implementation practices. Without both, the real business value is not achieved and your relationships with your stakeholders becomes compromised. Witold Henisz emphasizes that developing strong relationships with key stakeholders is not simply about good PR or corporate spin. It is actually about the broader goals of the organization and should be closely integrated into the operational performance of the business. Increasingly, organizations that ignore this do so at their own peril.

Felicity Fouche, Independent Strategic Communications and Stakeholder Engagement Consultant; formerly with AngloGold Ashanti & Rio Tinto

It seems common sense, but to view yourself from the perspective of your stakeholders can show you things you simply cannot see. Effective and meaningful stakeholder engagement relies on sound analysis and people engaging people about issues they care about. *Corporate Diplomacy* provides example after example of the value of the process of building good relationships and the cost of getting it wrong.

Nicholas Cotts, Group Executive Environment and Social Responsibility, Newmont Mining Corporation

Henisz's *Corporate Diplomacy* offers a rare multi-disciplinary guide far beyond social license. The innovative tools and simplified checklists are accessible to staff at all levels. Data, dynamics and internal engagement summarize much experiential learning from the past decade. As we open our companies to more enduring external engagement, we have to be intentional and aware of our own internal cultures and communication styles. ... Armed with the lessons from this book, I expect the next generation of corporate diplomats to catapult us forward so that extractive industries, in particular, may better serve people, planet and profit.
Veronica Nyhan Jones, Extractives Sector Lead, Strategic Community Investment/CommDev, Sustainable Business Advisory, International Finance Corporation

It contributes new insights and methods to the subject of stakeholder engagement in an original and highly readable way.
Robert Boutilier, President and Founder of Stakeholder 360; author, *A Stakeholder Approach to Issues Management* **and** *Stakeholder Politics: Social Capital, Sustainable Development and the Corporation*

This book is a refreshing perspective on how stakeholder engagement can move beyond simple PR and sentimental aspirations to a practice that creates real value for all involved. Witold Henisz effectively uses real examples to demonstrate why shareholder value and public benefit are inherently intertwined. From there he provides readers with the practical tools needed to develop winning corporate diplomatic strategies.
Eric Kacou, Co-founder, ESPartners; author, *Entrepreneurial Solutions for Prosperity in BOP Markets*

In *Corporate Diplomacy* Witold Henisz draws from years of experience in the trenches – and he shares his insights in colorful stories about companies around the world who succeed or fail depending on their ability to engage with their stakeholders. The story of the privatization of power supply in the post-communist Republic of Georgia reads like a thriller and does not provide easy answers. But drawing from this and other experiences, Henisz develops a comprehensive and practical approach to guide those tasked with corporate diplomacy in their work. This book is full of concrete approaches that can help companies improve their interactions with various stakeholders. And it shows clearly that, for sustained success, it is not enough to look inside the organization, improving production and internal processes. A company that fails to engage in corporate diplomacy risks angering their neighbors, regulators and other stakeholders – who can severely damage the organization and, in the worst case, drive it into bankruptcy.
Eva Schiffer, Leadership Trainer, The World Bank

Corporate Diplomacy spells out the business sense of strategically building relationships with stakeholders. Its case studies are a useful reference in the search for ways to continually improve this crucial area of business.
Yedwa Simelane, Executive Vice President, Stakeholder Relations & Marketing, AngloGold Ashanti

Corporate Diplomacy
Building Reputations and Relationships
with External Stakeholders

CORPORATE DIPLOMACY

Building Reputations and **Relationships** with External Stakeholders

WITOLD J. HENISZ

Greenleaf
PUBLISHING

© 2014 Greenleaf Publishing Limited

Published by Greenleaf Publishing Limited
Aizlewood's Mill
Nursery Street
Sheffield S3 8GG
UK
www.greenleaf-publishing.com

Cover by LaliAbril.com

Printed in the UK on environmentally friendly, acid-free paper
from managed forests by CPI Group (UK) Ltd, Croydon

British Library Cataloguing in Publication Data:
A catalogue record for this book is available from the British Library.

ISBN-13: 978-1-78353-055-7 [hardback]
ISBN-13: 978-1-78353-056-4 [PDF ebook]
ISBN-13: 978-1-78353-140-0 [ePub ebook]

~

To
the corporate diplomats who inspire me with their journey
my students who aspire to follow them
Marcia, Sophie and Katya for making our own journey

~

Contents

Acknowledgments

This book is a synopsis of a more than decade-long journey, with, hopefully, more decades to come. I owe a real debt to all of the practitioners and students who have shared their perspectives and experiences with me along the way, and those who I hope will do so in the future. I owe particular gratitude to Bennet Zelner my long-standing co-author, co-principal and co-conspirator; Sinziana Dorobantu and Lite Nartey whose combination of grit, insight and inspiration brought hard-edged academic rigor to previously abstract and ill-defined arguments around the material benefit of stakeholder engagement; Robert Boutilier whose Stakeholder360 process helped Bennet and me translate our academic insights into practice; Felicity Fouche, Matthew Chadwick, Laurent Coche, Anders Arvidsson, Nathan Monash and Cory Brandt for, in turn, supervising our work at the Continental African Region of AngloGold Ashanti; Robert Court and Judy Brown for the opportunity to help design and implement the Stakeholder Engagement Academy at Rio Tinto; Nick Cotts, Veronica Nyhan Jones and Arjun Bhalla for their cooperation and support in the development of the Newmont Ahafo teaching case and introduction into the IFC Sustainability Exchange community; the late Claire Missanelli and all the interviewees she introduced me to that informed the development of the AES-Telasi case; Richard

Young, Alan Hill, Dragos Tanase, Gabriel Matauan, John Aston and Stephanie Roth and all of their colleagues for their cooperation in the development of the Rosia Montana teaching case; Chris Anderson, Mamadou Beye, Vincent Blais, Richard Boele, Ian Bremmer, David Brereton, Alex Burger, Allison Coppel, Chris Coulter, Jeffrey Davidson, Philip Deardon, Shaun Doherty, Mark Edleson, Sebastian Escarrer, Steven Fox, Ben Heineman, Maria Figueroa Kupcu, Cameron Hume, Paul Kapelus, Alan Kelly, Adam Lees, Nick Lovegrove, Mary Matthews, Thibaut Millet, Ovais Naqvi, Francois Philppart, Scott Poynton, Jon Samuel, Eva Schiffer, Houston Spencer, Ian Thomson, Esther Trujillo, Paul Warner and all the others who have taken the time to speak with me, share their perspectives and shape my vision of the best practice of corporate diplomacy.

I must also thank all the academics in political science, economics, sociology, psychology and management whose theories, frameworks and approaches to related problems have helped me organize these experiences into practical tools. The interdisciplinary environment and intellectual integrity of the Management Department at The Wharton School have afforded me the freedom to explore this broad terrain. In addition, I should acknowledge the debt of specific chapters to the following previously published work.

- INTRODUCTION. This is an excerpted version of a three-part teaching case and accompanying teaching note[1]

- DUE DILIGENCE. This chapter draws upon joint consulting work with Robert Boutilier of Stakeholder360 process and his previously published books.[2] I also drew insight from the work of Eva Schiffer[3]

- INTEGRATION. This chapter draws upon an in-process teaching case developed in cooperation with Newmont Mining Corporation and the International Finance Corporation (IFC)[4] as well as a consulting engagement with EY. Thanks to Nick Cotts, Veronica Nyhan Jones, the staff of Newmont Ahafo and

Thibaut Millet and his team at EY. I also drew insight from the work of Bob Willard[5]

- PERSONAL. This chapter draws both upon the work of Sherry Arnstein,[6] and Luc Zandvliet and Mary Anderson,[7] as noted, and also the case studies on community participation developed by Rachel Davis under the supervision of John Ruggie and currently available through www.shiftproject.org[8]

- LEARNING. The subsection of this chapter on dynamics draws upon behavioral traps noted by Daniel Diermeier[9]

- OPENNESS. This chapter draws upon the work of Daniel Diermeier[10] and Alan Kelly[11]

- MINDSET. This chapter draws on Harrison Miller Trice's and Janice Beyer's typology of rites[12]

Finally, thanks to Tim Gray for tightening my prose and making it more accessible, as well as to Joel Carino for his copy-editing and formatting assistance both with the book and associated web portal.

Preface

Corporate diplomacy creates real business value. It is not just feel-good atmospherics or canny PR. This book provides a mix of colorful examples, practical tools and perspective on a fundamental challenge that managers of multinational corporations face as they strive to compete in the 21st century. Managers are struggling to win the strategic competition for the hearts and minds of external stakeholders. These stakeholders differ fundamentally from managers in their worldview, their understanding of the market economy, and their aspirations and fears. Yet their collective opinions of multinational corporations shape the competitive landscape of the global economy.

As communication costs fall, shrinking the distance between external stakeholders, shareholder value is increasingly created and protected through a strategic integration of the stakeholder-facing functions. These include governmental affairs, stakeholder relations, sustainability, enterprise risk management, community relations and corporate communications. Through such integration, the place where business, politics and society collide need not be a source of nasty surprises or unexpected expenses. Instead, by elevating corporate diplomacy to the executive level, and applying sophisticated management tools, multinational firms can create value for shareholders and society.

Part of the obstacle to realizing this vision is that many managers do not view the corporate functions that contribute to diplomacy as central to their company's mission. Thus, corporate diplomats have lower status and less clout than colleagues in operations, finance and marketing. Furthermore, staffers in the functions that contribute to diplomacy, such as government affairs, communications and community relations, tend to spar with each other, which further undermines their clout.

This book offers, for the first time, a framework that integrates these various functions and gives corporate diplomats tools to increase their effectiveness and status within their companies. But understand that doing this requires moving beyond the moral suasion that typically dominates diplomacy discussions, and embracing quantitative, data-driven decision-making. It was only when marketers adopted more rigorous techniques that they moved from the corporate periphery to the core. I offer a new foundation for diplomacy—a scientific approach that can shift the balance of power within a company in a manner that highlights the strategic importance of external stakeholders.

The analytic tools that I provide here can identify external stakeholders, and the issues they care about, and pinpoint which of these issues offer the greatest potential for financial gains and losses. Implementing a corporate diplomatic strategy then requires melding of this analytic approach with a traditional one steeped in an understanding of human behavior and the cultivation of personal relationships. Relationships do still matter, and they must be nurtured in a manner that builds trust. The inevitable conflicts must be managed in a manner that does not damage relationships. Goals and achievements must be communicated, and all members of the organization must believe in, and support, these inter-related elements. The challenge is to integrate these two approaches rather than set them in opposition. Data and analytical insight then can guide conduct in the field. I aim to give you the framework to achieve that.

I provide examples of success and failure that highlight six elements of best practice: Due Diligence; Integration; Personal; Learning; Openness; and Mindset—DIPLOM for short. Two of these elements (i.e., Due Diligence and Integration) are data driven and analytic. They will appeal to engineers and financiers. The remaining four are behavioral, with two focused on implementation within the firm (i.e., Learning and Mindset) and two focused on implementation with external stakeholders (i.e., Personal and Openness). These will resonate more with the sustainability and community affairs practitioners. Each of the book's main chapters focuses on a separate element, providing lessons learned by other companies and practical tools for your company, non-profit or government agency. I often refer to "companies" and "firms" in the book, though the elements can also serve non-governmental organizations (NGOs) and government agencies. In the conclusion, I discuss the challenges of moving forward on all six elements simultaneously and why so few, if any, firms have succeeded in doing so.

The framework rests upon a foundation of social science, spanning disciplines from political science to corporate finance. But I stress practical insights, not academic theories. My goal is not just to help you understand the political and social milieu in which your firm operates, but also to provide tools to enable you to protect, create and capture value. What I have written is an introduction, not the final word. Readers who want to explore further are encouraged to access the corporate diplomacy web portal (www.corporatediplomacy.com), where the cases described here are provided in greater detail. The portal also provides an evolving library of tools and examples, and a venue for practitioners to share insights and experiences.

Most of the firms profiled here are at the frontier of one or more elements of corporate diplomacy. But they did not start there. Many were motivated by past failings. They fell into conflicts with critical stakeholders—politicians, communities, NGO staffers, or activists—and they suffered. They experienced delays or disruptions to their operations, higher costs, angry customers, or thwarted attempts at expansion. At first, they stumbled and bumbled, and some of their initial reactions created unrealistic expectations on the part of stakeholders, leading to even higher costs or nastier conflicts.

Eventually, these companies developed smarter strategies for stakeholder engagement. They became corporate diplomats. I draw on their experiences to take you to the forefront of stakeholder engagement and to highlight six elements of corporate diplomacy (see Fig. 1).

Figure 1 **The six elements of corporate DIPLOMacy**

These elements are as follows:

- DUE DILIGENCE. Corporate diplomacy begins with a deep analysis of stakeholders and what they want. Absent that, managers are left with little more than guesses. Just as an oil field or gold mine begins with an analysis of geological and engineering studies, so must corporate diplomacy rest upon a foundation of stakeholder analysis. A smart manager or team must identify the stakeholders (that is, outsiders who have a financial interest in the project or who care about it for political or ideological reasons), the resources they control, and the reasons the project matters to them. This information can come from traditional sources, such as surveys, or social media monitoring. These data are the foundation for a stakeholder engagement plan

- INTEGRATION. Stakeholder data must be integrated into a firm's broader business. A corporate diplomat has to secure the buy-in from colleagues in departments such as finance and marketing. An engagement effort will likely fail if, say, your CFO thinks it is a waste of money

- PERSONAL. Corporate diplomacy reaches beyond the technical, calculating and analytical to incorporate interpersonal skills. A financial settlement can fail not only because it is cheap but also if it is offered grudgingly. Stakeholders should perceive a firm's actions as having resulted from a transparent process in which everyone, both the powerful and the powerless, had a voice. They should see a firm that respects everyone's views, rather than just ruthlessly chasing its own interests. Disputes will always arise, and they should be managed using conflict resolution techniques such as conciliation and arbitration

- LEARNING. Corporate diplomats adapt and change based on feedback from stakeholders. No plan or strategy is perfect, and none can be static. People's power and preferences vary over time, as do political and economic conditions. Put differently, "decide, announce, defend" (DAD) is dead. The old-fashioned approach to stakeholder engagement was to decide on a plan, announce it to the world as a fait accompli, and defend it against all comers. Such an approach no longer works—if it ever really did. A savvy firm solicits feedback upfront and adapts. This does not mean that it always agrees or accedes. But it tries to understand and anticipate objections, not just react to them. Ideally, the firm can engage opponents up-front, demonstrate its empathy and understanding by changing its plan to address legitimate claims and grievances, and thereby trigger a similar shift to a compromise position by the opposition

- OPENNESS. Perceptions matter. If stakeholders believe that your company is a secretive bully, then you become one—every interaction gets interpreted within that frame. The best way to head off that kind of perception is through a culture of openness. Openness entails conveying information in a manner that reinforces trust and reputation, ensures accountability and creates realistic expectations

- MINDSET. Corporate diplomacy requires a new way of thinking within corporations. Everyone, from top executives to entry-level workers, should recognize that short-term financial wins can lead to medium- to long-term political losses, which, in the long run, end up being more costly. Without the right mindset, the interactions between a few employees and external stakeholders can undermine a firm's overall goals. Achieving this collective vision requires ongoing training and corporate communications that feature diplomacy as prominently as other central corporate values, such as safety, customer orientation and innovation.

I did not invent the term "corporate diplomacy." It has been used by a small number of practitioners and consultants, including Michael Watkins, a professor at IMD in Switzerland, who defines it as:

> The role senior executives play in advancing the corporate interest by negotiating and creating alliances with key external players including governments, analysts, the media and non-governmental organizations.[13]

Most large multinationals and non-profits today employ parts of the approach that Watkins describes, but, even within a single firm, the practitioners can work in a sort of corporate solitary confinement—isolated from each other and able to communicate in only the most rudimentary ways. Companies have governmental affairs staffers who meet with politicians, regulators and community leaders. They have marketing teams, which track media mentions, customer satisfaction and marketplace trends. They have communications offices that interact with investors and reporters. They have human resources offices that encourage employees to contribute to communities in which the firm operates. Yet each of these activities happens with limited, if any, coordination. As a result, when these corporate diplomats have to compete for scarce money or personnel, they are unable to justify their requests with the same precision as peers. They are dismissed as representing the soft side of business or a cost center, when, in reality, they represent a creator of value that is starved for data.

Executives in many companies perceive what I call corporate diplomacy solely as philanthropy or image polishing. In these old-fashioned firms, managers in charge of stakeholder engagement often frame the need for diplomacy in terms of reputation enhancement. And they often fail to address a critical question: how much is enough? The answer cannot be to sacrifice every dollar of shareholder profit to be perceived as a white knight. Companies have to balance competing demands and protect their shareholders' wealth. Rather than introduce "triple bottom line accounting" or some other arbitrary target, they must incorporate stakeholder engagement into broader calculations of shareholder value.

Another impediment to corporate diplomacy is inertia. Managers in, say, finance or operations are not used to considering external stakeholders when they make decisions and weigh projects. They sometimes dismiss peers who lack their kinds of analytical skills. Similarly, staffers in corporate communications or governmental affairs may see themselves as lonely teams tasked with narrow jobs, such as improving awareness of the brand or securing an exemption from a regulation, rather than key parts of a broader enterprise. Harnessing such diverse perspectives within a company can be an exercise in diplomacy as difficult as engaging with NGOs, communities and government officials, and as equally important.

In today's interconnected world, the successful implementation of the six elements of corporate diplomacy will matter in an ever-larger group of companies. As more firms operate in emerging markets, differences in human rights, labor rights, environmental regulations and values across countries will affect their operations in unexpected ways. On top of this, technology has given external stakeholders greater power and reach: mobile phones and the internet enable a single person to capture an iconic image, post it on Facebook or YouTube, and broadcast it to the world. Likewise, stakeholders can more readily organize their actions to put pressure on companies.

In 2009, a long-standing poll by the Pew Charitable Trusts captured a collapse in public confidence in the profession of management.[14] Over the course of half a century, the percentage of respondents who perceived management to be a profession that "contributes a lot to society's well-being" had slid to 21%, which was last place out of ten professions (the others being artists, clergy, doctors, journalists, lawyers, military, scientists, engineers and teachers) in 2009. Analogously, the percentage of people who ranked management as a profession that "contributes not much or nothing to society's well-being" had climbed to the top spot with 31%.

Other surveys, such as the Edelman Trust Barometer,[15] have reinforced this finding, suggesting that society has come to expect more from companies than short-term profit maximization. Mind you, I am not suggesting that meeting those sorts of expectations is easy, or that trying to do so does not risk failure. But ignoring them, I believe, courts even bigger, costlier failures. To show how that can happen, the introduction to this book describes a case of utter failure in the Republic of Georgia. In offering it, my goal is to draw attention to the risks of not paying enough attention to corporate diplomacy. I then move to chapters detailing the six elements of corporate diplomacy supported by examples of successes drawn from multiple economic sectors and a wide array of emerging and developed markets—gold mines in Africa and Europe, construction projects in Asia and the

US, hotels in Latin America, and military campaigns in the Middle East and Central Asia. The successes of the corporate diplomacy framework in these far-flung locales highlight that the social license to operate is more than rhetoric. It is strategically relevant. And they show that becoming a corporate diplomat is not just corporate social responsibility. It is enlightened self-interest.

Introduction:
Power trip or power play: the case of AES-Telasi[16]

> With investments like this you first go through a honeymoon period. Everyone thinks you've shown up with suitcases full of cash and are going to solve all of their problems. Then you have to lay people off and raise prices. Next you're just focused on not getting hurt. Once the rumor starts that you're leaving, the sharks really start swirling around you.
>
> —Expatriate former employee of
> AES-Telasi

As Michael Scholey shifted his weight on the canvas bags of carrots that filled the back seat of a battered car, he could not help but wonder if his efforts to bring power to Tbilisi, the capital of the Republic of Georgia, were destined for naught.

It had been a tough first year. Early on, his project—the expansion by American Energy Services (AES) into Georgia—had seemed so promising. He had started off by negotiating an agreement to import 120 MW of electricity from Armenia, which provided a few hours of light to his customers in Tbilisi on New Year's Eve, 1999. The Georgians had loved that. Since then, he had confronted little but frustration—corrupt officials, rampant electricity thievery, and a local power distribution network so antiquated and unreliable that it could only operate for a few hours a day. Now, on top of it all, he was enduring this—a midnight ride atop a lumpy bag of carrots.

His journey back to Tbilisi, already eight hours long and far from done, had begun at an airport in Armenia—or it was supposed to have begun there. He had missed both of the daily flights and had had to hire a private car. The driver had insisted on stopping off at home for dinner, and they had arrived late at the border. The driver then refused to continue until morning. Considering this an underhanded demand for more money, Scholey jumped out and negotiated another ride. The catch: the carrots. After this driver, too, stopped at home for dinner—this time close to midnight—they finally began the descent from the border back to Tbilisi. Scholey dozed off but then awoke, with a start, when the car conked out at 3 o'clock in the morning.

Now, as Scholey peered into the darkness, his mind cast back over the tumult of the last year. He had arrived in January 1999, as the new president of AES-Telasi. From the start, he had known that he faced a challenge in trying to turn around the company that AES had acquired—an ill-equipped former Soviet electricity distributor serving 370,000 customers in a country with an average income of $600 a year. The distributor should have served even more people—Tbilisi's population was more than a million—but electricity theft was rampant. The lack of customers may, however, have been a blessing. The distributor, known as Telasi, could not handle the weak demand it was seeing, on account of its antiquated equipment and Georgia's rickety electricity generation network. Blackouts happened regularly, sometimes daily, and the country had to import up to 30% of its power and natural gas from its less-than-reliable neighbors, including the big bear to the north, Russia. And the bear snarled unpredictably: the Russians liked to bully their Georgian neighbors by snapping off the power when they did not get what they wanted.

Thus, from the first day on the job, Scholey had been improvising. Little he had learned as a geologist or an accountant—he had trained as both—prepared him for Georgia.

AES Corporation

At the time of its acquisition of Telasi in December 1998, AES Corporation, based in Arlington, Virginia, was the largest independent power company in the world. It owned 24,076 MW of electricity-generating capacity and distributed power to 13.2 million people in five countries. It was expanding internationally—soon it would reach to 18.4 million customers in 11 countries. Throughout the expansion, President and CEO Dennis Bakke and Chairman Roger Sant had tried to maintain the nimbleness and informality of a smaller firm. "We abhor layers," Sant said. AES had no central marketing, finance or human resources departments. Local managers handled all of these tasks themselves. Only five organizational layers separated any employee from Bakke.[17]

The Republic of Georgia

Georgia lies between the Black and Caspian seas, with Russia muscling it from the north and Turkey squeezing it from the south. Its position athwart Europe and Asia has made control of its mountain passes strategically important for centuries. It was conquered, in turn, by the Romans, Persians, Turks, Mongols, Russians and Soviets. In the 1990s, the country's strategic importance was rising again due to the discovery of oil and gas deposits in the Caspian Sea, and a need to transport these supplies to European markets.

After gaining its independence in 1991, Georgia tried to sidestep Russian dominance by using US interest in its location to its advantage. Its efforts were rewarded with inflows of US aid, but Russia continued to lord its military might over its tiny neighbor. Thousands of Russian troops remained stationed at two military bases in Georgia. Russian interests extended into the economy, too, via offshore shell companies that funneled money to the Georgian mafia. Peter Mamradze, a top adviser to the Georgian president, lamented that "living next to Russia is like living on the slope of a volcano."[18]

Georgia had real economic potential. It had abundant rivers, forests, minerals and rich agricultural land, including fine vineyards. Its population was educated and familiar with Western culture. Its people had a firm sense of national identity. But corruption thwarted the country's quest for modernization and stability.

Georgian corruption was among the worst in the world,[19] pervading almost every aspect of life. University students had to pay bribes for admission and exam grades, and police extorted money from drivers on the highway between Tbilisi and the airport. Two-thirds of transactions took[20] place in the gray or black markets. The World Bank estimated that, in 1998, an amount equal to 75% of the government budget was lost due to non-payment of taxes. Tax collectors often purchased their positions and then granted exemptions to people who paid them big enough bribes. Senior government officials consorted with smugglers. Finance Minister Guram Absandze was accused of embezzling $18m and conspiracy to assassinate President Shevardnadze.[21] The corruption was so severe that, in December 1998, the International Monetary Fund (IMF) suspended Georgia from membership and limited the country's access to multilateral funds.[22]

AES's case for investing in Georgia

When the IMF walked away, Georgia's need for outside investment in its electricity system was becoming desperate. The sector ran financial deficits that swamped the country's otherwise improving fiscal position. Losses totaled between $250 million and $400 million annually, equivalent to roughly 7.5% to 15% of the country's gross domestic product at the time.

The electricity system had been crippled by neglect. At best, less than half of the country's power plants were available to make electricity.[23] Brownouts and blackouts happened daily. Theft was another bedevilment. Many people stole electricity using illegal lines tapped into the transmission system.[24] The government could not cut the illegal lines because it had installed few meters and often could not distinguish legitimate users from scofflaws. Where meters did exist, meter readers often demanded bribes from consumers to underreport usage, and diesel fuel meant to run power plants in the winter was routinely sold on the black market.[25] Of the $82 million in foreign aid received for power sector reform, $15 million disappeared.[26]

The unreliability of the country's fuel supply compounded the problems. Georgia depended on hydroelectric generation, powered by its rivers, making it especially vulnerable in dry years. Neighboring states were often unwilling to help by providing power. Due to the Georgian government's weak finances, neighbors did not trust that they would be paid. In November 1994, Turkmenistan, to which Georgia owed $400 million for natural gas and power, severed supplies.[27] Four years later, the Russians claimed unpaid debts of $500 million for fuel oil, gas and electricity imports.[28]

Electricity shortages damped economic growth and stoked social unrest. Foreign firms were afraid to invest in Georgia for fear that they could not secure enough electricity. Each winter, the population grew restive, as the hours with power supply dwindled to the low single digits. Georgian politicians may have been corrupt, but they were not stupid—they knew that their country needed reliable electricity, and they believed that a foreign power company could help them provide it.

Foreign interest in Georgian power sector reform

Western donors tried to help. Hundreds of millions of dollars in aid flowed from the US, Germany, Sweden, the UK, Canada, Greece, the Netherlands, Turkey and dozens of NGOs. In response, Georgia attempted to reform its electricity sector. A new regulatory agency was established in 1997, and entry rules for foreign companies were liberalized in 1999.

AES enters Georgia: AES-Telasi

AES was one of the first Western firms to arrive. The Georgian government had announced plans to privatize Telasi, the distribution company serving households in and around Tbilisi. AES Director General Paul Stinson first formally raised the prospect of AES's entry—along with the hopes of Tbilisi residents—in October 1998. That December, Georgia's then president, Eduard Shevardnadze, in a radio address, proclaimed: "Electricity will be supplied to the population 24 hours a day, in the event that payments are made promptly."[29] Meanwhile, the official who negotiated the privatization said: "By selling Telasi to the US company AES, there will be an end to the dark nights."[30]

AES offered $25.5 million for 75% of Telasi, with the rest being owned by the government or employees, plus $10.35 million for partial debt repayment to the government. The company also committed to invest $22.6 million in the first year and $84 million over ten years. It promised to install a computerized collection system, allowing consumers to pay their bills through local banks or payment offices rather than having to hand money to bribe-seeking meter readers.[31] The government, in turn, met virtually every one of AES's contractual demands. It even agreed that the two parties would arbitrate any disputes in London, in English, using the English text of their agreement. An analyst summarized the deal thusly: "If you believed the contract, AES was guaranteed a 20% return on its investment."

On 22 December 1998, the Georgian government announced that it would pass ownership of Telasi to AES as of 4 January 1999.

The leadership team

Control over AES-Telasi was assigned to the manager who had identified the opportunity and made the case for the purchase—Michael Scholey. Journalist Wendell Steavenson wrote of Scholey's qualifications for the challenge:

Scholey was a bluff laconic Yorkshireman, intelligent and tough, with one eyebrow that went up and one that went down. He was perpetually tired because there was so much work to do. He chain-smoked. When I first met him, he was laughing about the size of the rats in the toilets at Telasi and how bringing electricity to Georgia was a challenge like climbing mountains and exploring deep Africa was a challenge a hundred years before.[32]

One of many challenges Scholey faced was the inexperience of his management team, particularly with respect to running a distribution company and operating in a post-Soviet republic. In an off-the-record interview, an ex-employee recounted the downside of AES's decentralized hiring practices to me:

When AES posts an employee position in Tbilisi, who applies? We're not getting tier-1 applicants here. The company couldn't get anyone to apply. It is not part of the career track. … There was no support from headquarters for us, either. There were no medical benefits or a family relocation policy. There [was] no school, and no one to call when we were having problems.

Another ex-employee concurred: "We didn't have the quality of the staff we needed. We weren't used to 400,000 customers."

Litter on the floor, flooding in the basement

The day he arrived in AES-Telasi's headquarters, Scholey found litter on the floors and flooding in the basement. An enterprising outsider had set up shop selling ice cream on the second floor—without first asking permission. The office's single computer was dedicated to processing payroll; billing records were being inked by hand in ledgers. Needless to say, those records were unreliable. As Scholey and his staff pieced them together, they discovered that the official collection rate of 40% was wildly overstated: Only one in ten customers was paying for electricity. Even paying customers often had a second, even a third, illegal line pulling power from someone whose service could not be terminated. Households close to a hospital in the Matsminda neighborhood, for example, were notorious for enjoying the most reliable power supply in the city, despite payment rates of close to zero. Industrial customers, such as the Azota chemical complex, were just as unwilling to pay—their unpaid bills totaled $10 million.

The government compounded these woes by taxing AES based on the quantity of electricity distributed, not the amount paid for.[33] And money was not the only resource in short supply. Due to a fire in a hydroelectric plant in late December 1998, Scholey also faced a 300 MW electricity shortfall in his first week. Power was available for, at most, one hour a day in Tbilisi.[34] Scholey had to upgrade the company's equipment, including installing meters for every household. Without reliable power and reliable payments, no progress would happen.

With the aid of a trove of cash from headquarters, Scholey and his team invested heavily in improvements. They had little choice. AES had that contract with the government. If it did not upgrade, it would breach it. Scholey also wanted to show Georgians that AES would deliver on its promises. He was sure that, if he could provide reliable electricity, he would create an upwelling of goodwill—and give Georgians a reason to start paying for power.

The tally for Scholey's spending rose fast. In 1999 alone, AES exceeded its expected investment commitments for its first decade in Tbilisi. Lots of money was going out. Little was coming in. The biggest investments involved the meters. AES contracted with Black and Veatch, an engineering and construction company, to install them. At first, Black and Veatch put the meters in building basements, but that made them easy to access and tamper with. So it then resorted to locating them outdoors in locked metal boxes. That pushed up the cost of the metering and delayed its completion—the installations would not be complete until summer 2001.[35] By December 1999, meters were being installed at a cost of $75 apiece for 500 apartments a week, with a goal of 5,000 apartments a week by mid-May 2000.[36]

AES rehabilitated 37 high-voltage substations (costing approximately $100,000 each), 76 high-voltage transformers (costing roughly $40,000–$70,000 each), and 2,500 transformers (costing approximately $500 each).[37] As required by regulation, AES also provided the grounding to the city's electrical system, which the state-owned company had never completed.

In October 1999, Scholey also took steps to wean his company off imported electricity and fuel by purchasing Units 9 and 10 of the Tbilisi State Power Plant for $16.5 million plus a commitment to pay $2 million in back wages and invest $100 million. He also secured control of two hydroelectric plants under a 25-year management contract. He hoped that, by controlling AES's power generation, he could alleviate winter electricity shortages.[38]

All of the work was complicated by the fact that AES had too many employees and too little productivity. So Scholey laid off 700 workers. For goodwill's sake he did so generously, offering severance deals that included more than a year's worth of wages, money for job training, and payouts for unused vacation days and wage debts owed by AES's predecessor company.[39]

Many of the meter readers stole by reporting smaller payments to the company than they received from customers. Or they, too, tampered with meters to hide real levels of usage. The graft made meter reading lucrative, and some of the most educated and capable staffers were out in the field reading meters.[40] Corruption was so rife that employees were demanding bribes from each other—so meter installers would offer to install shorts that would make meters count only half the electricity consumed, and other meter readers would then demand bribes not to report the transgression. An employee at another regional distribution company in Georgia recounted how AES-Telasi warehouse employees offered to sell him meters at a bargain price. Similar rackets involved company computers, cell phones, digital cameras and video cameras.

In an incident that became part of company lore, Scholey responded with controlled rage. When his landlady showed him that she had paid the equivalent of a \$60 (120 lari) monthly bill but that her meter reader had booked only the equivalent of \$10 (20 lari), he called an emergency press conference at his home to fire the meter reader.[41]

Public relations

In June 1999, Scholey hired a full-time spokesperson and began to try to use the media to convince Georgians of the necessary link between payment and their power supply. AES started to run TV ads, and Scholey appeared on TV programs many nights. Electricity, he explained, was like bread—if you didn't pay, you didn't eat. He took part in live debates with government officials. He spent a day reading meters. He even confronted complainers, one by one. If there was a public protest or if an argument flared in the billing office, he would appear. Scholey thus became a recognized face in Tbilisi, to the point of even being satirized in a nightly TV cartoon.

AES-Telasi's investments, especially those in meters, were close to paying off by 2001. Within a few months, the company would be able to identify non-payers and suspend their electricity. Internal corruption began to abate, too, partly due to managerial ingenuity. Managers began to regularly rotate meter readers, limiting their opportunities for rigging meters and soliciting bribes. One regional manager fired all of his readers and replaced them with elderly women. He reasoned they would be more honest and might be afraid to tamper with meters.

AES, in contrast, was making little progress in its tangle with the Georgian government over unpaid bills. Subtracting the amount of state-owned companies' unpaid electricity bills from AES's tax bill led the government, in turn, to seize AES-Telasi's bank accounts. That prompted Scholey to terminate supply to agencies such as the Tbilisi metro,[42] the Supreme Court, and the ministries of economics, industry, defense, state property management and interior.

AES's fights with its suppliers also raged on. Each time the supply to Tbilisi stabilized, the Russians seemed to snap off the power, blackening both the city and AES's reputation for reliability.

The government rejected such AES-Telasi proposals as flat-rate pricing to apartments that had not yet been metered[43] and the termination of supply to industrial consumers that had not paid 50% of their bills during the past year.[44] Scholey scrambled to find ways to shore up AES-Telasi's finances.

Up against the gun

In the fall of 2001, Scholey left to lead the AES regional office in Turkey. As he packed his office in Georgia, he knew that, despite some victories, his tenure could hardly be deemed a success. Some of his regional managers had managed remarkable feats, bringing collections up to 85% or more, far above the breakeven point of 70%. But that alone would not ensure AES's viability in Georgia. AES's investments had outstripped all projections. The company had spent more than twice as much in its first two years—$190 million—as it had planned to invest over a decade.[45] According to the most optimistic financial models, AES-Telasi would generate its first annual economic profit only in 2009. Given the stock market crash in June 2001, and AES's operating losses in Brazil and other emerging markets during that same year, Scholey was not sure that his successor would be afforded that much time. He also did not know whether his successor could overcome the corruption that still afflicted the company every day. "We are up against the gun, and receive virtually no support from Georgia's alleged international friends to get over crisis after crisis," he said.[46]

Scholey's replacement was Ignacio Iribarren, who arrived in the fall of 2001. Iribarren had worked for AES in Venezuela and El Salvador and was no stranger to the challenges of emerging markets. But he did not share Scholey's belief in winning over employees and customers. He focused exclusively on the bottom line. His goal, he said, was to instill "in the people the belief ... [that] the ultimate goal of the business was to maximize AES shareholders' return on their invested capital."[47] AES-Telasi's finances would improve under Iribarren, but relations with government officials and the Georgian people would sour.

The hardline and the bottom line

Iribarren suspended all new investments that did not lead to immediate cash margin improvements. He refused to pay suppliers who had not paid AES-Telasi for electricity. He set employees against each other in service of what he called "creative tension." Here is how he described his approach:

> One major tactic ... was to place people with opposing incentives into situations where they must resolve differences and work together to move forward results ... You run faster when a dog is chasing you.[48]

Morale plummeted as cooperation and socializing among staffers collapsed. "He was just not able to motivate employees," one person recalled. "He could be quite abrasive. It was a total disaster."

Another casualty of Iribarren's cost-cutting was Scholey's outreach, which Iribarren dismissed as "non-value adding." He opted for a different approach:

> We focused our efforts only on those external affairs and regulatory and political bodies that had direct revenue relevance to the company's position in Georgia and to the economics of the business. We also reviewed the historical support we had received from our political allies and screened the truly committed ones from pseudo-supporters. For example, it had become clear that the US embassy was just about the only true supporter, whereas other perceived allied such as the [World Bank], [European Bank for Reconstruction and Development], and other international financial institutions were simply useless.[49]

AES-Telasi and the government hold off growing opposition

Iribarren demanded that the Georgian government tax the company only on its income, not its billings, and that it approve an electricity rate increase of 130%.[50] He threatened a lawsuit if the government did not accede. He accelerated efforts to cut power to non-payers, including the national meteorological station,[51] a kindergarten and a defense ministry hospital.[52]

His tactics succeeded at first. The government amended the tax law, charging AES only for sums actually paid by consumers.[53] It also approved monthly access fees and higher electricity rates.[54]

The price increases, however, sparked public protests and complaints from representatives of parliament,[55] the Tbilisi City Council[56] and the United Trade Unions of Georgia.[57] The government promised to increase electricity subsidies for those in financial need.[58] But that did not placate members of parliament. They demanded an investigation by the country's antitrust regulator,[59] which temporarily suspended AES-Telasi's rate increase.[60] A parliamentary commission concluded that the company's investments and expenditures in excess of those in the original contract should not be compensated by rate increases.[61] That contradicted the contract's explicit wording, but the argument carried weight with politicians and the public. Popular protests grew in late November 2001, as Tbilisi again endured widespread outages.[62] Parliament opened an investigation into allegations that AES-Telasi had lied about its investments to justify increased rates.[63]

Iribarren responded by seeking greater direct control of the electricity sector and more help from the executive branch. He demanded that AES-Telasi employees be stationed at the government's electricity dispatch centers, empowered to intervene if workers tried to provide power to delinquent firms.[64] He also sought an increase in state subsidies to needy Georgians and compensation for the 15 days during which AES-Telasi's rate increases had been suspended. The government complied and,[65] within a week, also sent its energy minister to Moscow to negotiate a new fuel supply contract with the Russians.[66]

AES-Telasi's focus on the bottom line loses government support

Emboldened, Iribarren doubled down in his campaign against delinquency. He cut power to the state chancellery, parliament and other state agencies on 12 December 2001;[67] to the Tbilisi mayor's office and water pumping station on the following day;[68] and to the defense, state security and interior ministries on the day after that.[69]

Amid the hostilities, one of AES-Telasi's two electric generating units exploded.[70] The cause of the blast could not be identified, but Iribarren's decision to let almost all of his experienced engineers take a Christmas holiday could not have helped. AES could not offset the loss solely through the import of Russian or Armenian power, and Tbilisi once again faced a cold, dark winter.

Iribarren further inflamed his critics by using the workers freed up from operating the damaged plant to cut illegal private lines.[71] The opposition Labour Party began to refer to AES as "an American occupier" and sued to annul the privatization of Telasi.[72] Workers in the state-owned transmission and dispatch centers went on strike. The stalemate stretched into spring and then summer. Iribarren refused to back down, and Georgians grew ever angrier.

Then, on 14 August 2002, the CFO of AES-Telasi, Niko Lominadze, was found murdered in his apartment. He had been bound and shot in the head. Soon afterwards, a police officer threatened to kill another employee, reminding him of what had happened to Lominadze. Two other employees were beaten by police.[73] A bomb exploded at a billing center.[74] Iribarren himself received an anonymous death threat,[75] leading him to evacuate his family from the country and move into a suite at the Marriott Hotel.

As a second winter loomed, blackouts remained a bane for AES and Tbilisi. One even occurred during a high profile soccer match between the Georgian and Russian national teams. Blame, of course, landed on AES.

The opposition Labour Party started an ad campaign urging consumers not to pay their bills at all.[76] Enough people responded that

AES-Telasi was deprived of funds to buy gas from the Russians[77] or pay its taxes for 2002.[78] The Georgian government stepped in and bought the gas on the company's behalf, but this move met opposition in parliament.[79] So the government shifted its position and announced its intent to rescind the most recent electricity rate increase, leading AES to sue in London for a violation of the privatization agreement.[80] The leader of the Georgian Labour Party called for Iribarren's arrest.[81]

Then, in March 2003, the Georgian government seized AES's bank account for non-payment of taxes[82] and released the chief suspect in the murder of the company's CFO.[83] With the transmission line from Russia down due to an armed attack by Russian-sympathizing separatists, and AES-Telasi unable to pay for Armenian imports due to the seizure of its bank account, Tbilisi residents faced blackouts extending into the spring of 2003.

The cycle of charges and countercharges, bluffs and blackouts, culminated with the arrest of AES-Telasi's new CFO on charges of fraud. Within weeks, AES replaced Iribarren and paid $34 million to leave the country. A Russian firm, RAO-UES, bought Telasi's assets for $26 million, and AES paid off the European Bank for Reconstruction and Development and IFC debt of $60 million. AES shareholders were left with a loss of approximately $300 million.

A few months later, the Shevardnadze government fell in the Rose Revolution. The protests began in Tbilisi and soon spread to all of Georgia's larger cities. In January 2004, the head of the opposition, an American-educated lawyer named Mikheil Saakashvili, ran unopposed for the presidency and claimed 94% of the vote.

Fools or visionaries?

Were Scholey and his bosses in the US foolish to enter Georgia—a corrupt country with a crumbling electricity system and scant experience with democracy? Perhaps, but only a few months after the company's departure, the Rose Revolution burst forth, and the subsequent privatization of a Telasi sister company, Relasi, proceeded with far less confrontation. Better corporate diplomacy might have helped AES survive long enough to succeed in this new environment. Application of the corporate diplomacy framework suggests that a better understanding of Georgia and more astute engagement could have made the difference.

Due diligence

AES entered Georgia without a formal stakeholder plan or even a detailed analysis of its prospective customers. Its managers did not appreciate Russia's opposition to US ownership of the electricity transmission system. "The Russians never liked US involvement in the Georgian energy sector," one person says. "It was a visceral reaction. They haven't given up the Cold War."

The AES managers also did not understand the tenuousness of President Shevardnadze's control—they had assumed his support would translate into influence over ministers, legislators and regulators. In reality, Georgian politics was as much in flux as its electricity industry.

"AES was naïve and blind," one stakeholder recalls. "Month after month, year after year, they found out things went wrong that they should have foreseen, from corruption to politics." Even worse, AES had no sense of how it was seen by average Georgians, who had not paid for power during the decades of communist rule. AES arrived with a Western expectation that people would see the link between their payments and reliable service. When customers did not pay, AES started leveling demands and then strong-arming them by cutting off power. "People believed that everything was theirs and that the new government was selling their property to foreigners," an observer says. "They didn't understand why the foreign investors were needed."

Integration

With both Scholey's spending and Iribarren's strong-arming, AES failed to take into account long-term costs and benefits, opportunities and perils. "They should have thrown less money at the problem in the beginning and faced up to the fact that the government turned to them not to save the country but to save money," a stakeholder says. "They were viewed by Georgians as someone to help them out financially. For a century, Georgians have been partying at someone else's expense, and they did it again."

Personal

Local expectations regarding AES's ability to quickly deliver reliable, cheap electricity were unrealistic. Scholey not only failed to confront these false expectations, he actively cultivated them when doing so was helpful to his efforts to enter the market. That set the company up for battles with disgruntled customers when blackouts continued. In response, Scholey relied on lobbying senior officials and appearing in the media, but did not cultivate a broad network of contacts, including, for example, members of the skeptical Labour Party. "[AES] needed a grassroots effort, not Mike Scholey on TV," one person says. And any trust that Scholey did build was squandered by Iribarren, with his taste for confrontation.

Learning

Throughout its time in Georgia, AES responded to problems by doubling down—on its spending, on its advertising and, later, on its much-publicized power cut-offs to high-profile non-payers. It tried blandishments first and bullying later, but never reassessed its strategy and adapted. Or, if it did, everything it learned was lost when Scholey left for Turkey and Iribarren replaced him. Iribarren squandered the goodwill that Scholey had created. His tenure was like the

Dark Ages: AES lost all of the hard-won knowledge it had gained over prior years.

Openness

AES limited its communications to the mass media; and Iribarren cut even that, reinforcing distrust. AES-Telasi may have been an electricity distribution company, but its inability to succeed in Georgia sprang from politics and perceptions, not engineering smarts or technological innovation. Neither Scholey nor Iribarren grasped that. Plus, as one critic notes, the ad campaign overlooked an obvious problem: "AES was running television commercials telling people to pay their bills, but there was no electricity. So how are customers going to get the message?"

Mindset

AES's rejection of hierarchy, and insistence on employee autonomy, was suited neither to a country that had only recently emerged from decades of communism nor to employees with little training or experience with Western business practices. If anything, AES-Telasi functioned as a business school for its best people. "For Georgia, AES's investment is a big success—not that they left but what they left," one person says. "They created middle managers. Previously there were no business people, only bureaucrats." But empowerment and autonomy also invited corrupt workers to continue their bad behavior. "The management style of devolution of responsibility in an environment of rampant corruption is a recipe for a disaster," another observer says. "You can't just assume that you can export a management style around the world."

AES-Telasi's misadventure in Georgia shows the financial and human costs of devoting insufficient attention to corporate diplomacy. AES was, at the time of its arrival, the largest private generator of electricity in the world. Yet it was outmatched by the complexity of a tiny country—by the stubbornness of the tradition of not paying for electricity, by the resistance of the people to an outsider, by the enduring corruption, by the machinations of the Russians. And AES's experience is not an isolated story of mistakes by one cocky American firm. Rather, it epitomizes failures experienced by high-profile multinationals across the world. The corporate diplomacy framework emerged from my study of firms such as these, their mistakes and successes. My hope is that, through the application of the tools in each chapter of this book, readers will be able to avoid costly mistakes like those made by AES-Telasi. As a diplomat from an earlier age, Otto von Bismarck, famously quipped: "Only a fool learns from his mistakes. A wise man learns from those of others."

One

Due diligence:
Mapping and analysis of your stakeholders

D ue diligence, or the lack of it, doomed AES in Georgia. The company's mergers and acquisition staffers and its investment bankers undoubtedly vetted Telasi—they surely understood its low collection rate, its antiquated accounting systems and its rickety distribution network. They also probably appreciated the scope, if not the precise extent, of the electricity thievery—the illegal lines spider-webbed throughout Tbilisi. What they did not appear to factor into their plans were the Georgians themselves—their history, their habits and their expectations. AES's top management, both in Georgia and the US, did not seem to appreciate the tenuousness of Shevardnadze's power, the local suspicion of foreign multinationals, or Russian resentment of US incursion in a country tucked against its southern border. AES fancied itself a savior. Plenty of locals saw it as an invader.

This chapter offers a guide to a novel stakeholder mapping and analysis protocol—a synthesis of a number of existing tools that can help you understand the sorts of factions and forces that buffeted AES so badly in Georgia. These tools are built on data extracted from stakeholder surveys, media analysis, and historical and demographic research. The chapter shows how to aggregate and visualize that information so as to answer these critical questions:

- Which stakeholders matter most?

- Which grievances should I stress?

- Which stakeholders should I rely on to introduce me to others?

- How are stakeholders learning about me and how can I influence their opinions?

Once compiled, a stakeholder database lets you do scenario analysis or modeling to allow you to see not only the current stakeholder landscape, but also the likely future evolution of that landscape. Modeling allows for an examination of current trends and comparisons of hypothetical interventions.

Of course, no matter how good your stakeholder data and modeling, the personal side matters too. Think of it this way—perfectly placed name cards do not make a party. A charming and canny host does. Just as the host discretely reshuffles the name cards when someone brings an unexpected guest, you will have to modify your plans once you have begun operating in a new place. Learning and adaptation are always required. So is a communication strategy to introduce your firm to a new audience, publicize your plans and persuade people of your good intentions. A committed team of employees will be needed to execute those plans. Due Diligence is essential, but it is just one element of an integrated approach to corporate diplomacy.

Stakeholder data

Individual-level data

Who are your stakeholders?

Who should be included within your stakeholder database? The goal is to incorporate people or groups who have a stake in the outcome of your project, and who can influence its success or failure now or later.

Stakes may be direct—someone will get, say, money or a job; or indirect—he or she will receive benefits from another person or organization that benefits directly. Even when people are not affected in obvious ways, they may still care about the outcome. They may associate a project with any number of controversial topics such as imperialism, political favoritism, government intervention in the economy, the loss of traditional values or environmental degradation. Sometimes, their beliefs might not seem reasonable, but that will not make the holders any less convinced they are true.

The set of potential stakeholders can seem overwhelming. Screening based on *influence* is thus required. Include in your database any stakeholder who can ruin your day. That potential is a function of how much power stakeholders have and how much your project matters to them.

How powerful are your stakeholders independently?

Power seems straightforward—a company CEO has it, an unskilled worker does not. But quantifying it poses difficulties. There is no objective unit of measurement, and people may differ in their perceptions. A laborer in the island nation of Tuvalu probably sees his prime minister as powerful; the CEO of Exxon Mobil may not. In the context of corporate diplomacy, the appropriate measure of power reflects the extent to which a stakeholder owns or controls resources that can influence a desired outcome or public opinion about that outcome. These resources include money, legal or political rights, and guns. They also include reputational assets and other sources of "soft power" that confer influence or status. The 14th Dalai Lama, Tenzin Gyatso, has little formal power, but many people, and not just Tibetans, see him as a moral leader of unusual probity and charisma.

Power does not lend itself to a single objective measure, so it is easier to consider it in relative terms—how does the power of one stakeholder compare with another? Who follows whose leadership? The goal is to assess the resources that an individual or organization has that can influence the success or failure of *any* project. Critically, this measure does not vary by project but is an overall score that should be equivalent for any given investment or project in that location. Contextual differences in power related to the nature of a proposal or due to the ability of one stakeholder to influence others are captured elsewhere.

Is a stakeholder's disposition towards the project cooperative or oppositional? Are your operations perceived as legitimate?

Like power, stakeholder position can be hard to define, but it is relatively easy to array stakeholders with respect to their degree of support or opposition for your work. Cooperation and conflict are signaled by words or actions. Pledging support and giving time, for example, signal cooperation, while condemning and protesting indicate conflict.

Some scholars and practitioners speak of the extent to which a firm, investor or policy-maker receives a *social license* from stakeholders. A social license is offered by a stakeholder when that person or group perceives you or your outfit as acceptable or legitimate at a moment in time. Social license is based on perceptions, not objective criteria, and, like a personal reputation for fair dealing or truth telling, it can be lost if it is not maintained. Its measurement requires canvassing the opinions of stakeholders.

How motivated are stakeholders by the opinions of their peers?

Some stakeholders may be resolute in their opposition, even in the face of pressure from their family, friends or allies. Others may be swayed by the opinions of peers. Someone's degree of independence can affect his or her role in a stakeholder network. Some stakeholders are more prone to jump to the majority, while others will stand fast even if they are the last holdout.

What issues matter to your stakeholders?

In developing an engagement strategy, you should understand what matters for each stakeholder. What do they value? What matters less to them? You may be able to bundle issues together in a manner that shifts the overall level of cooperation. If, for example, a stakeholder worries about environmental protection, addressing pollution may help. By contrast, influencing someone else may require attention to schools or healthcare.

Relational data

How strong are the connections between stakeholders?

Every stakeholder operates in a network of some sort—family, friends, neighbors, colleagues, co-religionists or political allies. Through these networks, stakeholders share information and resources and, at times, work together to achieve common goals. Understanding the structure of a network helps to identify key relationships and influencers—people who touch and can sway many others. For each stakeholder pair identified, your database should contain information on the strength of the particular stakeholder relationship (as compared to that between other stakeholder pairs), the kinds of connections between the stakeholders (financial, informational or social), their joint activities (political, work or social) and their typical means of communication (e.g., face-to-face conversations, phone calls, email, online social networks).

*Are relationships cooperative or conflictual? Do they afford each
other a social license?*

Using the same approach as described above, you can capture a stakeholder's disposition towards peers.

Summary of data structure

The resulting database includes a minimum of four fields for each
stakeholder (name, power, disposition and social influence), plus an
additional field for each stakeholder for each issue that matters to
that stakeholder (i.e., if there are ten issues in play and all matter
to everyone, there would be 14 fields per stakeholder). In addition,
there are two pieces of information on each stakeholder pair that
have a connection. The total data structure thus contains a maximum
of $4N + NI + 2N^2$ pieces of information where N = the number of
stakeholders and I = the number of issues. For a case of 100 stakeholders and 20 issues, the maximum number of fields is $(4 \times 100) +
(100 \times 20) + (2 \times 100 \times 100) = 400 + 2000 + 20,000 = 22,400$. Typically,
however, each stakeholder has preferences over only a fraction of the
issues and connections to only a fraction of their peers. If we assume
that each stakeholder has preferences on 25% of the total issues and
connections to 5% of their peers, we arrive at a more manageable
$(4 \times 100) + (100 \times 20 \times 0.25) + (2 \times 100 \times 100 \times 0.05) = 400 + 500 +
1000 = 1,900$ fields.

Data sources

Many sources can contribute to a shareholder database. Some can
be accessed quickly, such as news articles available online. Others,
like the information on social relationships, will require more time
and money to collect. Either way, reliability increases with effort
expended.

Expert assessments

In the easiest and quickest process, a small group of managers with knowledge of external stakeholders creates the database in a workshop over the course of a few hours. They draw on their experiences with stakeholders and their knowledge of media reports and other sources. The process may include a consultant or facilitator. It may also be informed by the report of an external consultant with expertise into relevant political and social dynamics. This approach relies upon the objectivity of the managers involved. They must accurately and dispassionately record information on stakeholders. Inasmuch as they do not, the database loses value.

A powerful tool to develop a quick analysis that minimizes bias has been developed by Eva Schiffer. Her Net-Map diagnostic tool[84] was developed when she was a post-doctoral fellow for the International Food Policy Research Institute working in rural Ghana with the Challenge Program on Water and Food. The process involves the literal mapping of stakeholders using figures whose varied heights represent their power. These are then linked with color-coded markers capturing different types of relationships. A group of internal experts and, possibly, external stakeholders can convene a workshop to quickly identify the pertinent inputs and create the map. The map itself, which is seen by all participants in the workshop, helps to identify biases and omissions while highlighting areas of disagreement among participants. Furthermore, the act of making it is itself a form of stakeholder engagement, which can help to build and maintain trust between the company and stakeholders. These benefits have been seen in the use of Net-Map in water projects in Ghana, Canada and Iraq; agricultural projects in Zambia, Uganda, Nigeria, Malawi, Kenya, Ethiopia and Brazil; women's health advocacy in Ethiopia, Malawi, Nigeria and India; nutrition policy in Bangladesh; development policy in Burundi; and environmental policy in the US.

In-depth stakeholder surveys

A common next step is a stakeholder survey conducted by employees or, preferably, external consultants. A typical questionnaire[85] would take 60 minutes per interviewee. A model, using as an example a mine and the community surrounding it, is provided in the box.

Model questionnaire

The interviewer describes the purpose of the survey and identifies the company or project sponsoring it.

Stakeholder-level data

Issues

1. Which are the most important concerns for your community/organization right now?
   a) Why is that important?
   b) Which is the most important aspect *to you*?

2. How does the project affect your group?
   a) Why is that important to you?
   b) Which is the most important aspect of that to you?

3. Which changes or improvements to the project would you like to see?
   a) Why is that important?
   b) Which is the most important aspect?

Social license

I am going to read 16 statements. Please tell me how much you agree or disagree with each. Answer using a scale from 1 to 5 where 1 means you strongly disagree, 2 means you disagree, 3 means you agree and disagree equally at the same time, 4 means you agree, and 5 means you strongly agree. If you don't know, you can say "I don't know" (DK).

1. Our community/organization is very satisfied with its relationship with the mine.

2. Our community/organization and the mine's personnel have a similar vision for the future of this region.

→

3. We need to cooperate with the company to reach our most important goals.

4. The company listens to us.

5. They do what they say in their relations with us.

6. They openly share information that matters to us.

7. We can gain from a relationship with them.

8. In the long term, the company makes a contribution to the well-being of the whole region.

9. The company gives more support to those who it hurts.

10. The company takes account of our interests.

11. The presence of the company is a benefit to us.

12. The company shares decision-making with us about things that affect us.

13. The company treats everyone fairly.

14. The company respects our way of doing things.

15. The company is concerned about our interests.

16. People here speak well of the company.

Cooperation/Conflict

17. Thinking about your organization's relationship with the company and the level of either cooperation or conflict in that relationship, which words would you use to describe your degree of conflict or cooperation?

18. Please describe any actions you have undertaken that demonstrate that level of conflict or cooperation with the company.

Issue salience or intensity of preferences

19. In an average month, how much of your organization's total time is spent dealing with issues related to the mine? Would it be none, less than half, over half, or about half?

20. If this line represents all of your organization's time and this mark represents half of the time, where would you draw a line to show how much time you spend on issues related to the company?

None	Half	All
	- -	- -	

Power

21. Which are the key organizations or groups that we should talk to in order to better understand your community's support for the mine (or lack thereof)? These can be local, regional or national groups.

Relational data (for each individual or organization listed in response to questions 5 and 6 plus some set of "core" stakeholders)

I am going to read four statements. Please tell me how much you agree or disagree with each. Answer using a scale from 1 to 5 where 1 means you strongly disagree, 2 means you disagree, 3 means you agree and disagree equally at the same time, 4 means you agree, and 5 means you strongly agree. If you don't know, you can say "I don't know" (DK).

22. There is no conflict between us. We have a very cooperative relationship with them.

23. Concerning things of mutual interest, to what extent do you agree with the company on goals for the future?

24. We coordinate our public actions or comments. They almost always consult with us before making any comments or taking any actions about the mine.

25. In our consultations, we almost always follow their guidance or leadership in deciding which actions to take or comments to make.

The answers to these questions can populate the database structure defined above.

- The issues matrix should be derived from the accumulated responses to questions 1–3 making efforts to group-related concepts and issues together to ensure comparability across stakeholders

- Stakeholder social license or cooperation/conflict scores can be derived from responses to questions 4–21
- The power of a given stakeholder can be estimated from the frequency with which they are mentioned in response to question 24 as well as through efforts to ensure that the responses to questions 27–28 across stakeholder dyads are transitive (i.e., stakeholders follow stakeholders with greater power and are followed by stakeholders with lower power)
- The disposition of one stakeholder towards another can be derived from the responses to questions 25–26 for that stakeholder dyad
- The strength of connection between two stakeholders can be derived from the responses to questions 27–28 for that stakeholder dyad
- Stakeholder preference dependence can be derived from the number of stakeholders for which questions 25–28 are answered

Beyond the choice of questions, ways to enhance the reliability of a survey include:

- Conducting surveys in privacy at a neutral or stakeholder site rather than using the web, the phone or one of your offices
- Employing interviewers who are fluent in the local language and customs—if ethnic, religious or factional tensions exist, the composition of the interview team should match, proportionally, the composition of the area
- Interviewing multiple representatives per stakeholder group

Surveys are costly. A way to save money is by conducting workshops in which you interview multiple stakeholders simultaneously or in quick sequence. Group interaction can also enhance mutual awareness and understanding. But this does not work in situations characterized by extreme conflict or polarization, where ensuring security without sacrificing reliability may be impractical. If yelling or fisticuffs might break out, you are better off spending more money and keeping people separate until a forum or meeting can be productive. One recent example comes from a roundtable on the Canariaco Mine in Peru in which ongoing disagreements around the validity of competing dialogue tables escalated to the point where opposition leader Gregorio Santos staged a walkout. His lieutenant stormed out and into an assembled group of opposition supporters who he had arranged to have present. In front of a group of sympathetic media reporters who he had also invited, he inflamed his supporters with the aim of coercing the remaining participants of the forum into recognizing an alternative forum for which he demanded recognition.

Media (traditional and social)

Traditional and social media can offer a wealth of complementary data if a project is big and newsworthy enough to generate coverage and comment. Analysts can be hired to comb through the media and extract "stakeholder events" (i.e., instances in which one stakeholder took an action or expressed a sentiment that conveyed conflict or cooperation towards another stakeholder). The source, verb and target can be coded for each stakeholder event with the verb classified on a conflict–cooperation scale. Findings then feed into the stakeholder database. Media reports and online comments offer more than just a record of who is for or against a project. Analysis of links between the authors of various online posts and comments can yield insights on:

- A stakeholder's power, derived from the frequency with which the media mentions the stakeholder

- A stakeholder's conflict–cooperation score; that is, a single number which summarizes someone's disposition toward a project

- The strength of connection between two stakeholders, derived from the frequency with which they are linked in stakeholder events

- The attitude of one stakeholder towards another, derived from the conflict–cooperation score for the stakeholder events that link them

According to Stephen J. Andriole, Vincent J. Schiavone, Erike von Hoyer, Mark D. Langsfield and Mark R. Harrington, authors of *Avoiding #FAIL: Mitigating Risk, Managing Threats and Protecting the Corporation in the Age of Social Media* and *Social Business Intelligence*, the frontier of social media monitoring, including their own offering of ListenLogic, can now meet the requirements above as well as being able to:

- Collect 100s of millions of data snippets daily

- Extract author and publisher information; harvest demographics and augment demographics through the use of statistical models and machine learning techniques

- Use machine learning techniques to continuously improve data filters

- Use lexical, semantic and statistical filters

- Classify, index and store 100s of millions of items/day in real time

- Integrate structured/filtered social media data into enterprise platforms

- Develop and validate explanatory and predictive models

- Contextualize conversations

- Develop "what-if"/"if-then" scenarios for real-time listening/engagement

- Develop an aligned social media return on investment (ROI) model

Other internal data

Many companies already have information on stakeholders' identities, power, positions, preferences and connections, but fail to link that information to engagement efforts. Complaints or grievances recorded in phone calls, emails or face-to-face conversations can be analyzed using techniques such as those described for media. Where those communications are made jointly or identically by multiple stakeholders, connections and cooperation can be inferred.

Useful tools and frameworks

Stakeholder typologies, issue prioritization and engagement strategies

Once a database is compiled, the next step is creating visual summaries and reports. The most common are stakeholder and issue prioritization matrixes, which examine the relative power of stakeholders and the salience to them of your project (see Fig. 2). A graphic like this draws attention to stakeholders in the upper right quadrant (i.e., high power and high salience), whose concerns should be addressed. Stakeholders in the lower left quadrant (i.e., low power and low salience) need not receive much attention. Those in the lower right (i.e., low power and high salience) should be kept informed, while greater effort should be devoted to satisfy those in the top left (i.e., high power and low salience).

In the AES-Telasi case, impoverished Georgians had a high interest in the case due to the high share of their income devoted to paying for electricity, but they had low power and little ability to influence the outcome. The Georgian industrial companies, who benefited from political influence to obtain free electricity, had high salience and high power. The US government had high power but limited salience as it was unwilling to antagonize Russia by meddling in Georgian politics. Finally, the European Union had both limited power and limited salience because none of its companies were directly involved in the dispute.

Figure 2 Stakeholder classification of power × salience

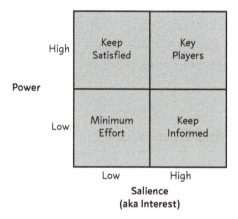

Based upon this analysis, one can generate issues matrixes, which prioritize issues according to the effective power (i.e., power × salience) score of the stakeholders who mentioned those issues.

In Figure 3, 12 issues are arrayed in rows with 11 categories of stakeholders arrayed in columns. The count of mentions of each issue in each cell is weighted so that mentions by stakeholders with greater effective power count more than mentions by stakeholders with lower power or salience. Comparing such an issue matrix to one based on raw counts alone highlights which issues matter more to key players according to the framework of Figure 2.

In Figure 3 you see a graphic constructed for a mine in Africa. When taking effective power into consideration, it highlights the importance to stakeholders of transportation infrastructure, land use, waste and unemployment. In the corresponding analysis, which ignored effective power and just counted issue mentions, sanitation/hygiene infrastructure and water would have appeared more important.

Figure 3 **Mentions of issues by stakeholder groups, weighted by effective power**

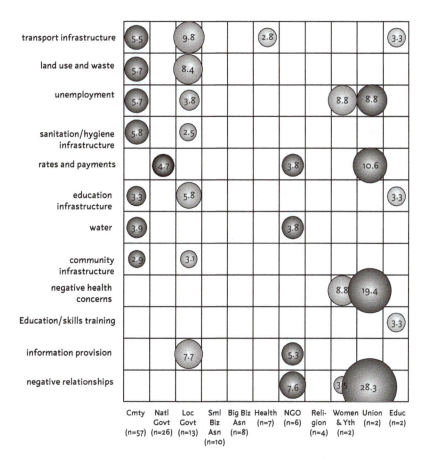

	Cmty (n=57)	Natl Govt (n=26)	Loc Govt (n=13)	Sml Biz Asn (n=10)	Big Biz Asn (n=8)	Health (n=7)	NGO (n=6)	Reli-gion (n=4)	Women & Yth (n=2)	Union (n=2)	Educ (n=2)
transport infrastructure	5.5	9.8			2.8						3.3
land use and waste	5.7	8.4									
unemployment	5.7	3.8							8.8	8.8	
sanitation/hygiene infrastructure	5.8	2.5									
rates and payments		4.7					3.8			10.6	
education infrastructure	3.3	5.8									3.3
water	3.9						3.8				
community infrastructure	2.9	3.1									
negative health concerns									8.8	19.4	
Education/skills training											3.3
information provision		7.7					5.3				
negative relationships							7.6		3.5	28.3	

Another typology, depicted in Figure 4, modifies the previous visual by plotting stakeholders according to their disposition toward your project—that is, the amount of social license they have granted you—on the horizontal axis and their effective power (i.e., power × salience) on the vertical axis. Stakeholders in the upper right quadrant (i.e., high power and high social license) represent influential allies who should be mobilized. Those in the bottom right quadrant (i.e., low power and high social license) are weak allies who should be assisted to build their capacity over time, making them more powerful. Weak opponents (i.e., in the bottom left quadrant) should be the target of persuasion through media and communications campaigns but not more person-to-person outreach. Strong opponents (i.e., in the top left quadrant) must be coopted through more consultation. This framework helps more in ranking issues than in guiding engagement efforts with different stakeholders.

Figure 4 **Stakeholder classification of effective power × social license**

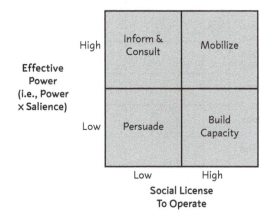

Another approach, developed by d'Herbemont and César (1998),[86] emphasizes salience and disposition. The results here are useful both for prioritizing issues and differentiating approaches for interacting with specific stakeholders. Their framework classifies stakeholders based on their salience and "antagonism"—which is simply the converse of the social license. "Cheerleaders" are stakeholders with the highest salience and support (i.e., low antagonism). Counterintuitively, your relationships with these stakeholders should be managed carefully so they do not damage your relationships with other stakeholders. Stakeholders in this category are blind to competing claims and so rabid in their support for you that their actions may alienate their peers. Examples might include union members in a mine or plant threatened by a shutdown due to environmental concerns. They might be willing to go to great lengths to keep the mine open, including even coercing or intimidating opponents.

"Bystanders" are stakeholders with low salience and high support. They are potential allies who are not engaged. These might include family members of workers or businesses who would benefit indirectly from a project. Bystanders should be consulted in a manner that gives them voice and treats them fairly, in the hope that the consultation and engagement will increase their salience.

"Disinterested skeptics" (i.e., low salience and moderately high supporters), in contrast, can be ignored. The effort required to make them any more than waverers is too high to justify the return. Examples of this category of stakeholder include members of a regional political party or interest group in another part of the country that broadly supports business but has not weighed in on your project.

Finally, "interrogators" and "challengers," who are stakeholders with moderate to high antagonism and low to moderate salience, must be overcome, but ideally in a manner that minimizes confrontation and resources lost. These groups form the core of the opposition due to the net financial costs that they incur if the project goes forward or due to their opposition to the issues with which the project is associated. Examples of stakeholders in these categories would include NGOs opposed to the project on environmental grounds and political parties seeking to embarrass a ruling government or prominent agency that supports a project.

"Supporters" are stakeholders with moderate to high salience and moderate to weak support. In contrast to the "cheerleaders," they should be given real responsibility and authority. Their independence and lack of zealousness when compared with cheerleaders make them ideal proxies for swaying waverers. Examples of supporters would include prominent business leaders who support the development and job opportunities associated with the project once they were convinced it met certain legal or procedural requirements. "Waverers" range from weak to moderately high in terms of salience, and from weak to moderate in terms of support. They are the undecideds on whom supporters and opponents focus their attention.

The final group is "opponents" (i.e., high salience but strongly opposed). They are the most unpredictable because they perceive themselves to have much at stake. Examples would include homeowners whose properties might be expropriated. Watch them carefully.

Issues matrixes that use these stakeholder groupings (see Fig. 5) can be helpful in identifying issues that link supporters and waverers (e.g., transport infrastructure, land use and waste, unemployment and sanitation/hygiene) or interrogators, challengers and waverers. These are the issues on which the battle for the hearts and minds of stakeholders should be fought. The common interest of challengers and opponents in water and community infrastructure is a cause for concern, as these issues could form the basis for an opposition coalition. The analysis can also reveal issues that matter to bystanders or disinterested skeptics, which, if addressed, could transform them into supporters.

Figure 5 **Mentions of issues by stakeholder types, weighted by effective power**

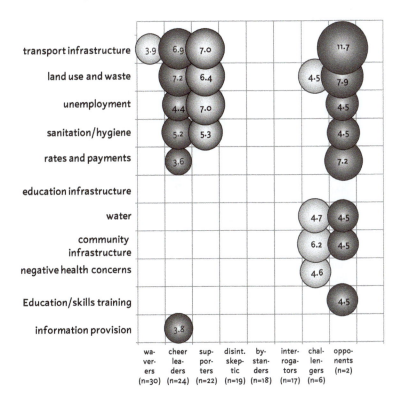

The d'Herbemont and César framework omits power. Though one could replot with power (i.e., power × salience) on the vertical axis, another option is to use a three-dimensional graphic that includes social license, power and salience. Murray-Webster and Simon (2006)[87] offer such a framework together with a categorization of eight stakeholder types, depicted in Figure 6.

Figure 6 Stakeholder classification of
power × salience × social license

Source: Adapted from Murray-Webster and Simon, "Making Sense of Stakeholder Mapping," *PM World Today* 8, (11, 2006): 1-5.

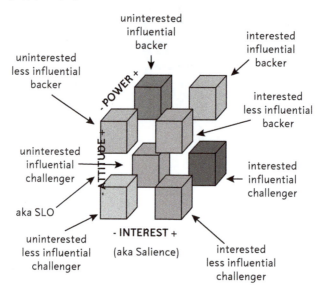

In their framework, "interested influential backers" (i.e., high power, high salience and high social license) demand attention, even pandering. "Interested less influential backers" (i.e., low power, high salience and high social license) are confidantes. "Interested influential challengers" (i.e., high power, high salience and low social license) should be coopted, if possible, to make them less active on their issues. If this fails, be prepared to adapt and clean up the mess they have created through their disruptions. Similarly, "interested less influential challengers" (low power, high salience and low social license) should also be engaged so that they do not erode the support of others. Another target for engagement is "uninterested influential backers" (i.e., high power, low salience and high social license) who, if activated, could become "interested influential backers." Keep "uninterested less influential backers" (i.e., low power, low salience and high social license) informed. Work to understand "uninterested influential challengers" (i.e., high power, low salience and low social license) so that you can defuse them before they become "interested influential challengers." Finally, work to understand "uninterested less influential challengers" (i.e., low power, low salience and low social license) to avoid unnecessary stumbles.

Once again, the issues matrix can be reproduced using this grouping with an eye for issues that are common across various groups and that, if addressed, could increase the coalition of supporters, weaken the coalition of opponents, mobilize supporters with low salience or neutralize opponents with high salience.

Each of these frameworks treats stakeholders as independent from each other, with the exception of the discussion of using supporters to sway waverers and the related risk that cheerleaders could push waverers away. The question of indirect pathways of engagement and sequences of interaction that build momentum for positive change are omitted from the analysis. An alternative set of tools sets aside or minimizes the visual importance of power, salience and disposition in favor of highlighting connections between stakeholders and the issues of importance to them.

Stakeholder and stakeholder-issue networks

The key to stakeholder engagement may not be *who* you engage first but *how* you reach the people you wish to engage first. Direct connections are not always best or even feasible. Relying on indirect connections, such as groups with common interests, respected figures, the media or other key influencers can sometimes work better than providing information directly. A press release might be seen as less credible than a news story, even when the news story repeats a lot of the information in the release—especially if someone influential links to the story on, say, his or her blog or Facebook page, and comments on it.

This kind of persuasion works because stakeholders' dispositions may be as much determined by what their peers tell them as their own observations. Social preferences have been shown to matter in a wide variety of seemingly individual decisions, including choices of friendship, relocation to a city, perceptions of class and corporate power, purchases of foreign products or services, acceptance of welfare support, the citation of work of other academics, reactions to natural disasters and what to post on social media and blogs.[88]

These indirect pathways of influence can be mapped as a network using your stakeholder database. A node in the network represents a stakeholder. The size of the node typically captures effective power and its color can show the stakeholder's type or disposition. You connect nodes with lines to signify connections or common issues of concern. Nodes with more connections are located closer than those with fewer connections.

Height (i.e., vertical position) in the graphs can sometimes be used to highlight stakeholders who have many connections to stakeholders who themselves have many connections. While this may seem like a complex characteristic and is, indeed, challenging to compute, it is the same calculation that is at the core of a search engine's page ranking or of Amazon's and iTunes's algorithms for making recommendations. They all derive information from the structure of relationships among nodes (websites, book purchases or song purchases) to generate insight into which website, book or song should be on top of the others in a search. Similarly, stakeholders at the top of such a figure are often opinion leaders.

The art in analyzing network graphs is in deciding which nodes and network segments to include. Including too many will create a spaghetti graph that is impossible to untangle and interpret. Including too few will omit important connections and limit insight.

In the example provided in Figure 7, the national police and the national health service are the two most influential stakeholders in the network, due to the large number of other stakeholders to whom they are tied, as well as the brokering role that each plays for otherwise unconnected groups. Tapping into the networks of these opinion leaders can be an effective means of communication for the investing firm. Working in cooperation with these opinion leaders can also broaden and deepen a coalition of support.

Figure 7 **Opinion leaders in a stakeholder network**

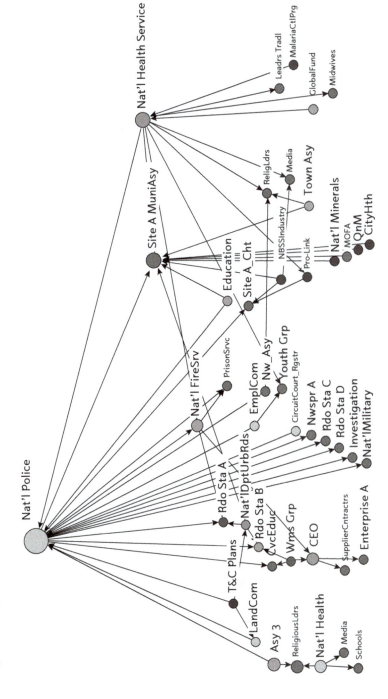

In Figure 8, we plot not stakeholders but *issues*. The lines indicate co-mentions (i.e., issues for which many stakeholders who mentioned one also mentioned the other). Issues closer to the left side were more commonly mentioned among stakeholders at one interview site (e.g., issues 2–7 and 11–14), whereas those closer to the right side were more commonly mentioned among stakeholders at another site (e.g., issues 1, 4, 8 and 9). This analysis helped to reveal differences in priorities by geography that would require some segmentation in the stakeholder engagement strategy.

Figure 8 **Issue co-mentions by interview site**

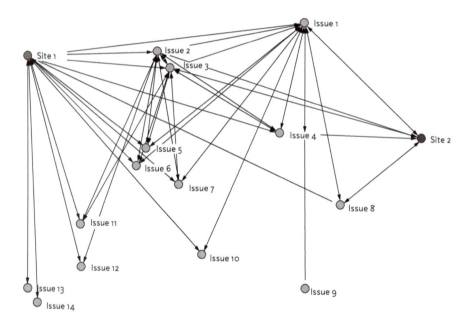

The final example is a graph with nodes for both stakeholders and issues. The two-mode graph in Figure 9 helps in identifying groups of stakeholders who share related concerns and could be mobilized together. For example, TownDAsy, TownEAsy, TownFUnit and ChfD share a concern on all four issues plotted, whereas TownX_QnM, TownDWmn and ChfF share concerns with land use and waste and unemployment.

As the number of issues and stakeholders increase, graphs like this can quickly degenerate into a scribble. One way to focus in on key connections is to plot only linkages that are strong or issues that exceed some threshold of importance.

The goal of any of these visualizations is to aid in the design and implementation of your engagement strategy. Imagine a visualization which reveals that one stakeholder is closely linked to several others. By focusing your communication efforts on switching the disposition of that one stakeholder you may be able to start a positive cascade, as they use their influence to persuade others to support your project.

In an example of this technique, consultant Robert Boutilier (2009) showed how to visualize opposition to the Antamina mine in Peru. His research[89] revealed that the opposition was rooted in 200-year-old familial disputes, and he convinced mine managers that their engagement strategy would have to change if they were to build relationships with opponents. His analysis showed that certain schools and universities acted as brokers between the factions. The company shifted its community development spending, which had been perceived to favor one group, to funding the schools supported by both.

Not all stakeholders matter equally. Stakeholders with many relationships, particularly if those relationships are with peers with many relationships, are good diffusers of information. Likewise, people who occupy positions between otherwise unconnected segments of a network can be key conduits.

Figure 9 **Co-mentions of issues**

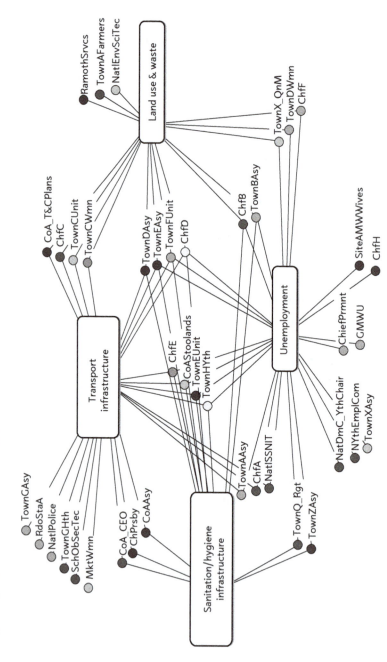

Figure 10 **Stakeholder network typologies**

Source: Boutilier, Robert (2011) *Stakeholder Issues Management* (Business Expert Press, New York).

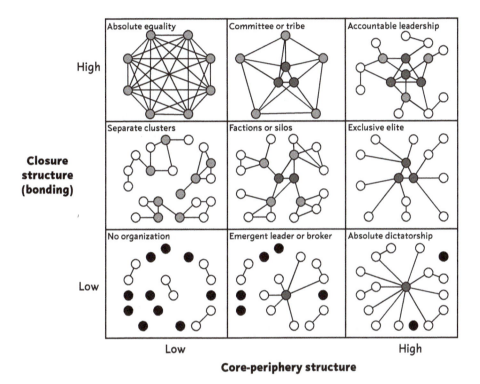

Understanding the overall structure of a network can also help in devising strategy. In his 2011 book *Stakeholder Issues Management*, Robert Boutilier has developed a typology of network structures (see Fig. 10). Along the horizontal axis, the typology moves from few relationships (i.e., low coordination/integration) between the core of the network structure and the periphery to many relationships (i.e., high coordination/integration). On the vertical axis, it moves from sparse ties (i.e., low accountability, information sharing and weak social structure) to dense ties (i.e., high accountability, information sharing and strong social structure). The typology includes nine prototypical network structures, each of which has its own strategic implications:

1. **No organization (i.e., sparse ties overall and few core periphery ties).** This is an unstable and unpredictable structure. It is most common among a group of stakeholders who have not seen a need to coordinate. From the corporation's perspective, any kind of organization might be preferable to the uncertainty stemming from this lack of structure

2. **Emergent leader/broker (i.e., sparse ties overall and moderate core periphery ties).** This is only slightly less unstable and unpredictable. Investors should resist the temptation to squash an emergent leader, even if his rallying cry appears inimical to their interests. The long-term benefits of enhancing coordination and information flow may offset the costs and risks. Companies often face such challenges when an opposition leader emerges and rallies and unifies previously unconnected or seemingly uninterested stakeholders into a more coherent and powerful force

3. **Perfect dictatorship (i.e., sparse ties overall and many core periphery ties).** While this structure may seem stable, the imbalance of power can make it fragile. Other stakeholders may try to topple the dictator, and the dictator may squash peripheral actors, sowing discontent. Efforts to help the leader recognize the benefit of addressing the needs of the periphery can enhance the stability of the system. Common examples of such structures are traditional power structures, which concentrate power in a chief or elder or religious leader

4. **Separate clusters (i.e., moderate ties overall and few core periphery ties).** This structure, often seen across regions or industries, is more stable and becomes problematic only as the number of issues that cut across clusters increases. As this happens, efforts to shift from tailoring engagement strategies to the particular demands of each cluster need to shift to efforts to forge interactions and linkages between clusters

5. **Silo organization (i.e., moderate ties overall and moderate core periphery ties).** This structure is among the most difficult to navigate as the silos are internally stable but prone to conflict with each other. Efforts to create a central coordination or control, while potentially beneficial to all, are likely to be opposed by people in silos prizing their autonomy and seeking to avoid connections to their peers who differ in religious, tribal or other affiliation

6. **Exclusive elite (i.e., moderate ties overall and many core periphery ties).** This structure resembles a dictatorship in its strategic implications. The added risk is that the trappings of more accountable leadership may dupe investors into thinking that the system is inclusive while, in fact, it is supported only by the elite. Again, efforts to help the leaders recognize the benefit of addressing the needs of the periphery can enhance stability. Common examples are groups with highly unequal political and economic systems in which voice and power are distributed among different groups but only those of high income or high political status

7. **Perfect equality (i.e., dense ties overall and few core periphery ties).** This structure is stable but typically small in scale and prone to groupthink and prejudice against outsiders. Efforts to broaden the group's perspective to foster greater trust for outsiders may help in mitigating future conflict. Examples would include local agricultural cooperatives or grassroots community organizations where work and authority are shared by all members

8. **Isolated tribe (i.e., dense ties overall and moderate core periphery ties).** This structure is stable but tends towards insularity. Consider the potential benefits of broadening the range of interests represented by the leadership. Examples of this organization would include larger scale cooperatives or NGOs that have delegated some authority to a leader

9. **Accountable leadership (i.e., dense ties overall and many core periphery ties).** This desired state is stable, inclusive and balanced with well-established rules and processes for collective action. Examples include companies or NGOs with well-developed corporate governance and representative democracies with high participation rates

Forecasting and scenario testing

Each of the visual tools and frameworks highlighted above uses a snapshot of data on the stakeholder network to aid in analysis and the eventual creation and execution of an engagement plan. But be aware that a stakeholder network is not static—it can change after the snapshot.

Thus insights can be gained by examining the evolution of the stakeholder map over time. Instead of a snapshot, imagine a series of PowerPoint slides consisting of stakeholder snapshots over months or years—the pictures change over time as the network changes. An engagement plan should look ahead and forecast how a network might evolve. Extrapolate from the past and use insights from the study of networks to improve the prediction. Models of coalition politics in political science can be used to anticipate the evolution of networks. Among the possibilities suggested by these models are the following:

- Where stakeholders have close links or care about similar issues, one stakeholder can "catch" a positive or negative disposition from another

- Relationships are likely to be reciprocal, so that when a stakeholder acts or speaks out, a linked stakeholder is likely to do so too, especially when the stakeholders share characteristics such as demographics or issue preferences

- Stakeholders may seek to form relationships with peers who are perceived positively and be repelled by those perceived negatively

- Stakeholders will seize positions as information brokers when they can, and these positions will make them more attractive partners for other stakeholders

- Stakeholders with many links to others will attract still more stakeholders who want to form relationships. But the challenge of getting their attention will lead to a diminishing return and enhance the attractiveness of ties to stakeholders with high but less extreme numbers of relationships

- Potential connections that form open triads (i.e., sets of three stakeholders, ABC, in which stakeholder A is connected to stakeholders B and C but stakeholders B and C are not connected) are more likely to be formed (i.e., B and C are likely to form a connection). The likelihood of such closure increases when stakeholders B and C share characteristics (i.e., demographics, issue preferences, other relationships).

- Within closed triads (i.e., sets of three stakeholders, ABC, in which all possible connections exist), ties are more likely to break among actors with differing characteristics (i.e., dissimilar demographics, issue preferences or relationships).

The application of rules such as these has been shown to assist in simulating the evolution of networks, including in classrooms, work and family groups, social structures, corporations and international trade exchanges, among others.[90]

These rules ignore the possibility that stakeholders are seeking to accomplish something within the network structure. Specifically, they omit the possibility that stakeholders may either champion or try to sabotage a project. Oddly, for an analysis of stakeholder network dynamics, the resulting model would not necessarily show a tendency for opponents to form ties or diffuse opinions that are more likely to forestall a project's development.

An alternative starting point for modeling stakeholder dynamics is to treat each actor as self-interested in the pursuit of some combination of achieving their preferred policy outcome and whether their coalition is on the winning or losing side. At any moment in time, each stakeholder can reach out to peers with an offer to move toward them and form a coalition. Each stakeholder's response to these offers is based upon the choice that he or she believes will maximize utility given expectations of every other stakeholder's actions. This scheme was developed by New York University political science professor Bruce Bueno de Mesquita[91] and, since being commercialized by Decision Insights and the Sentia Group, has been adopted by intelligence agencies, McKinsey[92] and the World Bank,[93] among others.

The next step is to forecast how one successful intervention might alter the evolution of the stakeholder network as compared with another. An example of this sort of analysis is a World Bank case study of an anti-corruption initiative in Mongolia.[94] The study revealed that, due to the ongoing election campaign, no feasible winning coalition could be formed to support the measure. As a result, the initiative was shelved to await a more politically opportune time.

By contrast, an analysis of a tax reform proposal in the Philippines led to a shift in strategy.[95] The analysis revealed that a public expression by the World Bank of willingness to compromise could weaken or gut reform. The World Bank therefore continued to publicly push for strong reform while signaling in private a willingness to compromise. This strategy had the effect of creating a winning coalition in the short-term while leaving the door open for greater reform in the future.

In my own recent research,[96] I have developed a framework that incorporates social preferences and social structure. In my model, a person's support for a candidate, for example, may be strengthened if his or her friends strongly support that candidate or weakened if they do not. Someone's social preferences can also be influenced by people who are similar, even in the absence of direct connections. If, for example, someone sees that fellow physicians or investment bankers support a candidate strongly, he or she might also support that candidate. In my approach, the power of any one stakeholder is not just a function of the resources controlled but also of network position— information brokers and people with many ties have more power.

Note that this is obviously not the way such stakeholders really interact. But the outcome, as in any good model, provides insight into, and mirrors, what may happen. The US Central Intelligence Agency (CIA) has subjected the core of the model to backwards testing and found that it generated valuable predictions on coalition dynamics and outcomes in over 90% of the cases analyzed as compared to alternatives.[97]

Diplomats' talking points and checklists

Corporate diplomats seeking to build support for the adoption of this approach, and questioned as to the nature of the likely payoff, can point to concrete examples in which companies have altered their strategies so as to:

- Shelve a major development project due to opposed groups' strong social cohesion and wide sphere of influence, together with fragmentation of the project's supporters

- Include a national government agency in a local stakeholder coalition to leverage the agency's multisectoral network

- Exploit a prominent ally's influence over rival media organizations to forestall a competitively driven cascade of negative coverage

- Expand a coalition of local supporters without appearing to undermine a powerful tribal leader's authority

- Forge a multilateral alliance including a local municipal authority and an international NGO

- Address legacy compensation issues of concern to a small but socially influential set of stakeholders

Had Michael Scholey and the management team of AES-Telasi had data such as these they might have recognized the critical

→

linkages between the industrial consumers of electricity and the Georgian government as well as Russia's jealously over US involvement in its former client state. After entry, they might have focused earlier and more aggressively on ensuring that the government's electricity distribution center was independently controlled. They also might have been confronted earlier with the need to curry favor with powerful political backers outside Georgia, including the US government, the European Union and international development agencies. The decision among these various strategies, and the amounts to invest in them, requires data on more than stakeholders. The next element of corporate diplomacy will link these data with the core financial and operational data of the business.

If you seek to deploy these tools in your organization, be sure to:

- Develop a stakeholder roster in a workshop or other brainstorming process:
  - Which organizations are directly impacted?
  - Which organizations are indirectly impacted?
  - Which organizations are motivated to involvement by issues?
- Gather data on each stakeholder organization
  - Variables should include
    » Power
    » Sentiment or social license to operate
    » Peer vs. self-orientation
    » Issue roster
    » Relationship to other stakeholders
      › Strength
      › Sentiment or social license to operate

- Sources of data to consider
  - » Workshop, brainstorming session or other Delphi technique
  - » Survey
  - » Media
    - › Traditional
    - › Social
  - » Other internal data (e.g., meeting minutes)
- Visualize data
  - Classifications of stakeholders
    - » Power × salience
    - » Power × social license to operate
    - » Salience × antagonism (i.e., 1 – social license to operate)
    - » Power × social license to operate × salience
  - Issue bubble charts
    - » Unweighted counts and counts weighted by salience × power
    - » Grouped by stakeholder type, geography and classification
  - Network
    - » Stakeholder
    - » Issue
    - » Stakeholder × issue
- Scenario test data

Two

Integration:
From stakeholder maps to financial and operational performance

To win workplace arguments you must quantify your evidence. Companies use discounted cash flow (DCF) analyses to evaluate potential investments, consumer surveys to assess new products and click-through studies to track online ad campaigns. Stories matter too—we humans are storytellers and make sense of the world by shaping facts into narratives. But stories alone will not convince colleagues—unless those stories are supported by numbers.

Corporate diplomats too often ignore numbers. They assume that moral appeals—"It's the right thing to do"—or dire prophecies— "We're repeating AES's mistakes in Georgia"—will sway colleagues. Those can help. Companies care about right and wrong, and we all learn from mistakes. But those alone will not beat spreadsheets, and they will not build companywide support for stakeholder engagement, especially in times of tight budgets. In an influential review of Newmont Mining's social responsibility practices, law firm Foley Hoag wrote that engagement is still seen as "voodoo" by professionals from other fields.[98] Marketing and human resources departments have embraced the tools of the social sciences to improve the precision of their analyses and to make their cases more convincing to colleagues. Corporate diplomats must follow, quantifying costs and benefits and providing credible estimates of how their programs can yield financial returns.

A DCF analysis is the standard way of making that sort of estimate. The term may seem forbidding, but anyone who can plug numbers into a spreadsheet and understand what those numbers mean can learn to do a DCF analysis. A day-long seminar will teach the basics. As a bonus, you will learn that the estimates emanating from the finance department are not as precise as they seem; the final number, positive or negative, depends partly on the assumptions. One of the key assumptions is where you draw the line on counting costs and benefits. It is simpler to look at direct short-term costs and benefits, and short-term estimates are typically more accurate.

In the construction industry, advocates of investing in energy conserving design and materials were originally stymied by a convention to focus the DCF analysis only on the period of construction and not on subsequent operation. Poorly insulated structures will typically be cheaper to build, but, on account of the greater need for air conditioning and heating, more costly to operate. Until the convention shifted from pricing buildings based on their lifetime operating costs, the green building movement struggled to go beyond principled rhetoric, while study after study showed that customers were choosing poor designs. The introduction of life-cycle cost accounting transformed practice, not because it changed the facts but because it empowered key decision-makers in finance and accounting to take those facts into consideration.

A similar revolution is underway in addressing the environmental costs of production of goods and services. Companies such as furniture maker Herman Miller, IT services provider SAP, and retailer Walmart, have found that efforts to reduce waste and resource use yield high economic and social returns. The Economist Intelligence Unit[99] highlighted the successes of these companies and others:

- Forrester Research found that Herman Miller's efforts to improve sustainability generated a 32% annual return on investment

- Walmart's calculations revealed that a 5% reduction in packaging would translate into $11 billion of cost savings, of which it would capture $4.3 billion

- 3M saved $1.7 billion through its pollution prevention pays (3Ps) program since it was introduced in 1975. The program seeks to prevent pollution upfront by reformulating products, manufacturing processes, redesigning equipment, and recycling and reusing waste from production

- FedEx aims to convert its entire 35,000 vehicle fleet to electric or hybrid engines. To date 20% have been converted, which has already reduced fuel consumption by over 50 million gallons

- Proctor & Gamble seeks to create an estimated $20 billion new product line in detergents that are effective in cold water

Jon Miller and Lucy Parker's powerful book *Everybody's Business: The Unlikely Story of How Big Business Can Fix the World*[100] highlights similar efforts by a number of companies to profitably address society's biggest problems. Among the case studies they examine are:

- Coca-Cola's development of a network of small-scale fruit suppliers across Africa, with the aim of supporting the company's continued growth while contributing to the emergence of the middle class in some of the world's poorest countries

- Nike's efforts to improve the monitoring of its supply chain to both enhance flexibility and deter the use of child labor among suppliers

- Mahindra's efforts to turn the brand position "Rise" into a profitable long-term oriented business model that serves the rising Indian middle class

- IBM's push to harness bid data, analytics, mobile technology and social business to allow for a "smarter planet, smarter industries and smarter cities"

- Unilever's and Nestlé's responses to accusations of environmental degradation caused by sourcing of non-sustainably produced palm oil

- MTN's embrace of novel distribution and pricing models to allow for communication services even in the most conflict-ridden, impoverished and infrastructure poor environments

- PepsiCo's efforts on both sustainable agricultural development and water conservation

- The embrace by BHP and Anglo American of the social license to operate as a strategic imperative

- GlaxoSmithKline's shift from suing copycat producers of its drugs to partnering with them to lower production costs, helped to generate political support for stronger intellectual property protection in emerging markets and identify new funding sources for drug discovery

These efforts were not corporate philanthropy; they were vital to the performance of the companies involved. Miller and Parker make clear that the managers of the companies they profile were able to transform their companies thanks to a combination of a serious threat to the business, clear potential benefits and strong internal leadership. How other firms might follow their examples is not so obvious. Not every company finds itself in dramatic straits, and not every company has the sort of charismatic managers who lend themselves to profiles. Broad-based adoption of the values and techniques that undergirded these successes will require not inspiration but perspiration—the inglorious, but essential, work of quantifying the benefits of corporate diplomacy.

Engagement professionals must embrace the DCF analyses they have long decried. But their DCF analyses will encompass not only longer (and thus more realistic) periods, but also secondary costs and benefits related to the stakeholders they have long championed. Skeptics will always argue that it is cheaper to ignore community complaints. They can do this successfully only if the data available shows short-term costs and ignores long-term benefits. Imagine a similar debate ten years ago at Walmart about reducing packaging or at FedEx about reducing fuel. Progress requires that someone makes a business case using the same tools and models that went into decisions to purchase computers, buy planes or build warehouses. Once corporate diplomats can calculate the likelihood of continued confrontation, and the costs and lost opportunities that confrontation brings, costs and benefits will look very different.

They can then break down the barrier between those who emphasize *share*holders and those who stress *stake*holders. One of the academics who has done the most to champion a shareholder focus within corporations is Michael Jensen of Harvard Business. Yet in a 2002 paper,[101] Jensen said: "We cannot maximize the long-term value of an organization if we ignore or mistreat any important constituency. We cannot create value without good relations with customers, employees, financial backers, suppliers, regulators and communities." He argued, though, that without a means to translate the costs of mistreatment into firm value, stakeholder theory fails to give concrete guidance to managers. Instead, he proposed "enlightened value maximization" as a decision-making criterion, and argued that it was identical to an "enlightened stakeholder theory." Jensen said that managers should "spend an additional dollar on any constituency provided the long-term value added to the firm from such expenditure is a dollar or more." In essence, the challenge that Jensen presented to corporate diplomats is how to incorporate stakeholder costs and benefits into the traditional DCF models, which omit them.

The IFC, in partnership with the Norwegian Ministry of Foreign Affairs, Deloitte, The Multilateral Investment Guarantee Authority (MIGA),

Rio Tinto and Newmont Mining, has developed a freely available online net present value (NPV) calculator that rises to the challenge posed by Jensen. It can be downloaded at www.fvtool.com.[102] In the rest of this chapter, I will explain how to gather the numbers that are the critical inputs for this kind of analysis.

Increasingly, evidence shows that numbers support the case for stakeholder engagement and that companies that ignore outside stakeholders do so at their peril. A 2009 Goldman Sachs study[103] examining the largest capital investment projects in the world highlighted that the time for new projects to be completed doubled between 1998 and 2008. More delays were caused by stakeholder and sustainability problems (70%) than commercial (63%) and technical (21%) ones. On average, the largest 230 projects in 2009 were 20 months behind schedule and 135% over budget compared with the 2006 forecasts for these same projects.

A 2012 Accenture study[104] of the projects in mining and metals likewise found that two-thirds were more than 25% over budget and that regulatory and stakeholder-related issues accounted for nearly half of the delays. Similarly, in a study[105] with Sinziana Dorobantu and Lite Nartey, I found that, for the 19 publicly traded gold-mining companies, the amount by which investors discounted the cash flow projections of a mine was highly correlated with the degree of stakeholder conflict or cooperation. We were able to estimate DCFs for the 26 mines owned by these companies. If investors and analysts had ignored stakeholder opinions, then the market capitalization of these firms should have equaled the NPV of their future cash flows.

What we found differed starkly. The average firm had a market capitalization equal to only 22% of its DCF projections. In other words, when these companies told investors that they had discovered gold that would generate $1 billion of new value, investors increased the companies' average market capitalization by only $220 million. Next, we coded over 20,000 newspaper articles, which contained over 50,000 reports of stakeholder actions or statements that connoted conflict or cooperation. We coded each of these stakeholder events on a conflict–cooperation scale and found that amount of the investor discount was strongly correlated with our conflict–cooperation measure. When we adjusted the DCF projections using our measure as a proxy for higher costs or lower revenues, we found that the investor discount ranged from a high of 99% for firms with the worst stakeholder conflict to as low as 13% for companies with the highest levels of stakeholder cooperation. This finding demonstrates that investors and analysts tracking a stock are monitoring the media and updating their estimates of cash flow, the opening dates of new mines, and company costs, based upon stakeholder actions covered in the press. The long-standing complaint by managers that investors do not pay attention to their efforts simply does not stand up. Our takeaway: any cash flow projection that does not incorporate the costs of stakeholder conflict is as inadequate as one that omits commercial or technical risks.

Gathering data needed for a DCF analysis is, of course, harder than talking about its importance. Doing so demands an upfront investment of scarce personnel time and requires support from bosses. But you do not have to do an exhaustive analysis on the first attempt. Start small, gathering the easy-to-quantify data and feeding that into the early estimates. Build from there. A 2013 Accenture study[106] surveying CEOs on sustainability highlights the potential benefits of even simple approaches: 63% of CEOs surveyed believed that sustainability would transform their industry within five years, and 76% believed that embedding sustainability into core business functions would drive revenue growth and new opportunities. *But* the CEOs also reported that they struggled to "quantify and capture the business value of sustainability." Thirty-seven per cent of them reported that this lack of a clear link to business value was hindering further action.

Among the readily quantifiable costs that you will want to include are:

- Direct costs, including staffing, capital investments and raw materials both initially and over a project's life

- Overheads or other hidden indirect costs

Also consider the less obvious cost reductions and revenue enhancements that a project might generate. Possibilities are:

- Revenue lost (gained) due to:
  - Lower (higher) consumer willingness to pay
  - Production stoppages or delays (accelerations in the timeline)
  - Ease of entry into markets due to new government regulations or policies that respond to opponents' (supporters') pressures

- Staffing expenses, including:
  - Managers to oversee engagements after a conflict
  - Engineers to redesign controversial plans and government affairs or regulatory staff to repermit after redesign
  - Guards to protect personnel and property when tempers flare
  - Lawyers and lobbyists to provide representation in proceedings or investigations
  - Higher training and recruitment costs as well as retention costs at corporate sites that have seen conflicts

- Insurance, risk management and compliance expenses, including fines and penalties

- Depreciation for property, plant and equipment (PP&E) that goes obsolete during delays and repairs for PP&E damaged during conflicts

- Higher PR expenses stemming from particular disputes

Many corporate diplomacy initiatives become easy to justify once their direct benefits and costs have been accurately measured and tracked. With accurate data, they become analogous to the well-known cases where expenses incurred in reducing waste delivered quick paybacks through lower costs for supplies, packaging and disposal. Many more corporate diplomacy initiatives may generate positive returns once their indirect benefits are considered, though indirect benefits will always be difficult to pin down.

When Newmont Mining used the FVTOOL at its Ahafo mine in Ghana,[107] its initial analysis focused on the cost and speed of land acquisition. The company had to not only compensate and resettle the people who lived or worked on the land that would be occupied by its mine, but it also needed to facilitate access to new land and the replacement of their livelihoods.

Newmont initially worked with planningAlliance, a Canadian urban planning and design firm with expertise in providing social assessment to natural resource companies. Together, they analyzed the number of people and amount of land affected, identifying 1,701 households, comprised of 9,575 people. These households owned 1,426 structures or sets of structures and eight businesses, and they cultivated 7,193 fields (2,426 hectares). Four schools, four sheds belonging to the Cocoa Marketing Board, two roads, and a system of tracks and paths, would also be displaced by the mine.

Newmont built two new villages—one called Ola Resettlement Village and another called Ntotoroso Resettlement Village. Both new villages saw rapid population growth on account of the new economic opportunities. Local authorities soon became concerned over the strain on local resources.

Newmont's external affairs team worked daily to ensure communication between the company and the communities. A special committee assisted with discussions and negotiations regarding resettlement. It consisted of: representatives from Newmont Ghana Gold Limited; the regional, district and traditional governments; NGOs; and the affected people. The committee helped to determine resettlement entitlements and also assisted with negotiations, earning the respect and trust of villagers. It was eventually replaced by a community liaison committee, which served as a link between one of Newmont's key agricultural programs and the new villages. The resettlement committee agreed that people would receive compensation if they had had a legitimate interest (not just ownership) in immoveable assets such as crops or buildings. In general, compensation consisted of a replacement residence and land plot, with the new home being equal in total area and kitchen size to the original. Residents could choose the colors of their new homes as well as the locations, and a group of neighbors could move together to retain their neighborhood. People also could opt for a lump sum of cash, instead of a new home, but only if they offered proof that they had an alternative residence outside of the mine area. About 424 households opted to leave. Public structures, such as the schools, were built in the resettlement villages. Overall, Newmont spent about $51 million on land access, including compensation, resettlement, livelihood restoration and vulnerable-people management.

In surveys, approximately 97% of the people affected by the mine said agriculture was central to their livelihood. Resettlement meant that farm families would lose land that they had cultivated and improved for years, even generations. It also could drive up land prices in surrounding areas and curtail production. As a result, Newmont developed and implemented a series of programs to help local farmers to re-establish their farms, boost production, diversify crops and enhance access to markets.

Experiences with Ahafo South led to a shift in focus in subsequent land acquisitions, with greater emphasis placed on negotiation and the priorities of residents. Newmont developed two programs—one for livelihood enhancement/empowerment and another for vulnerable peoples—intended to help affected communities. These programs were designed with significant local input and with the help of development NGOs and government agencies. They led to a perception that Newmont was a good neighbor and a fair and honest negotiator. As a result, land acquisition for the first expansion area to be developed beyond Ahafo South, called Amoma, was completed with an average payment of $2.87 per square foot less than the average in Ahafo South and $230,000 less in compensation for land and crops. More important, the process took four fewer months, allowing faster development of the mine. That translated to a $700,000 improvement in the NPV of the mine.

Another clear case of financial benefits was Newmont's malaria eradication program. In 2006, workers at Newmont Ahafo endured 3,195 cases of malaria, which led, on average, to three days of absence from work per worker. Given an average wage of $5 per hour this translated into $120 of paid wages without productivity as well as $30 worth of treatment, a cost of $150 per case—$479,250 overall. The company believed that the disease also hurt worker morale and led to reluctance to relocate to Ahafo. Newmont also provided care for workers' family members, and this expense was at least as large as the one for treating the workers themselves. In total the annual cost of malaria to the company ranged from a conservative estimate of $1,000,000 to a high of $2,000,000.

Faced with these costs, Newmont stepped up malaria prevention at its mine and in the villages, launching a $850,000 two-year control program. It distributed bed nets, instructed people on their use and supported community monitoring of bed-net usage. It also sprayed insecticide and improved drainage to eliminate insect breeding pools. These measures reduced malaria incidence in the community to near zero.

A similar analysis demonstrated that a $421,000 water treatment program, which led to a 30% to 40% reduction in the incidence of diarrhea, saved $1,120,000 in medical treatment costs.

A more complex set of calculations demonstrated the benefits of a program that invested $25,000 each in the training of 69 students in plant maintenance, electrical work and auto repair. Newmont had to compare the wages and salaries of these employees against those that it would have had to pay to people recruited from elsewhere in the country. The company also factored in the savings in recruitment costs (25% of annual wages) and evidence of lower turnover rates, which further reduced future recruiting costs.

In the rest of this chapter, I outline how to integrate stakeholder engagement into quantitative business planning to move from the realm of cases and stories such as these, where the financial benefits are clear and almost immediate, to quantitative analysis over a wide range of projects in which a richer comparison of DCF over the life of the project is required, including probabilistic estimates of the likelihood of certain risks or contingencies. The process begins with the education of the engagement staffers. They must learn to do cost estimates for their projects and then work to link their estimates with companywide budgeting and planning. Once they have learned the techniques, they will need to recruit a champion with real power within the firm—maybe the CFO, COO or a senior strategy executive. That person's buy-in is critical. An endorsement by someone who might be seen as a skeptic brings credibility. The best way to be taken seriously is to show that you are taken seriously by someone with real power. Together with that champion, you have to assemble a cross-functional team that either possesses or has the expertise necessary to estimate the data required as well as to communicate it effectively.

Understanding core business systems and processes

In the past, many corporate diplomats have operated in the equivalent of a satellite office. They may have shown up for work every day at the headquarters, but, except for occasional presentations and crisis interventions, they have been off by themselves. They focused on social and political objectives, and used language and techniques drawn from economic development and political science without linking those to the corporate world and, sometimes, even the corporation they work for. This divide, while natural, undermines stakeholder engagement. Bridging it begins with engagement professionals investing time in understanding core business systems.

How can a government affairs staffer with, say, a master's degree in public policy do that? Start by learning the data that top corporate managers monitor daily or weekly to assess performance and make strategic decisions. Key indicators vary by industry, but well-designed corporate dashboards share a focus on a set of measures that capture current and future performance. Typical metrics include:

- Net profit
- Return on capital
- Cash flow
- Expense ratios
- Health and safety metrics
- Capacity utilization
- Operational efficiency
- Customer satisfaction
- Waste generated and disposed
- Carbon emissions

You need to figure out which measures matter, learn what they mean and how they are used. Are in-house training programs offered that explain their use? Such skill building can deepen your understanding of your firm's incentives, its vocabulary for decision-making and the constraints faced by peers. On what basis do colleagues in other departments evaluate requests for more money or people, and how does that differ from the way in which the corporate diplomats make their evaluations? Knowing the answer to this question enables the construction of more persuasive arguments, just as understanding which metrics matter and what they say helps in avoiding ill-timed requests. It is foolish to ask for more staff during a cash crunch.

Integration with core business systems and processes

Sometimes, the links between engagement and a company's key metrics are obvious—for example, when shuttering a factory during a strike costs a company $1 million a day in payments to idle workers and lost revenue. Other times, sleuthing is required to identify and quantify connections.

Among the most frequently cited costs are delays and disruptions to supplies and operations as well as unanticipated material costs. In times of stress, these costs quickly mount, sapping operational performance and net profits. Having to source higher cost supplies due to turmoil is one example. If militants are blockading roads to protest your company's presence in their region, that is a failure of stakeholder engagement. If a civil war breaks out, that is not. Be credible in your claims.

As information is gathered, it should also be recorded in the stakeholder database and linked to the stakeholders responsible or priority issues. That information helps in assessing where to focus future engagement efforts. Understand that there may not be a one-to-one match between the grievances associated with a disruption and the stakeholders in the database and their particular complaints. Often, an accretion of complaints triggers a protest rather than a single incident. Sometimes, an unexpected or new problem can spark a reaction. In that case, the new topic should be mapped into the database and linked to the appropriate stakeholders.

During fact-finding, keep an ear open for additional costs or lost revenues resulting from stakeholder problems that might not have been obvious at the outset. Corporate diplomats often begin with an incomplete appreciation of the scope of costs and lost revenues resulting from stakeholder actions. Sometimes, the necessary information resides elsewhere in the company but has not been communicated or addressed in a systematic way. Instead, stakeholder conflicts and the costs of addressing them have been treated as one-off events and have not been analyzed with an aim of long-term mitigation.

Staff time devoted to conflicts and crises can be an example of this. If a company has to hire guards to protect a plant or mine, those additional wages probably stem from a failure of stakeholder engagement. Similarly, if hourly employees must work overtime to help to resolve a dispute, that imposes real costs. The challenge here is finding precise enough personnel records, since few companies track their employees' allocation of time by task—this many hours for compliance, this many for administration, this many for meeting with stakeholders, etc. But it may be possible to estimate the time allocated to a particular project or to resolving a particular stakeholder problem. The HR department will likely be the source of the best information.

Employment costs do not have to be limited to wages and salaries. In a region where malaria is endemic, investments in mosquito spraying, drainage, distribution of bed nets and education about their use might be set against reduced absenteeism and healthcare costs associated with malaria treatment. Similarly, investments in drainage and water supply can be set against similar savings due to a reduction in diarrheal diseases.

Information about risk management and compliance expenses is also usually readily available. The difficulty here is that some companies self-insure by not purchasing insurance for some kinds of risks and instead paying for problems as they arise. Whether this is smart—and cost effective—takes time and data to discern. You must compare the annual cost of insurance with the cost of occasional and often unexpected disruptions. The calculation requires estimating the expected costs of self-insurance using the methodology described here. This cost can then be compared against the cost of hedging or insuring.

The remaining categories of expenses or revenue are typically the most important—and the most difficult to measure. Like the risk management and compliance costs, budgets for communications and governmental and public affairs can be tempting targets for cost cutting, and the long-term financial impact of doing that can be difficult to estimate. HR staffers will know how much they will save in salaries if they halve the size of the communications department, but they will not know how much they could have saved by preventing strikes, protests and other sorts of disruptions. What is more, a sullied reputation can become a hefty cost if it leads to delays in regulatory approvals or the denial of permits. Thus, paying more for land compensation or to settle a claim may be worthwhile if you can show that it can reduce litigation costs and stem future delays to operations.

The idea that a less-than-stellar reputation imposes costs segues into the critical question of customer opinion and satisfaction. Some companies, such as mining firms, do not have to worry too much about quantifying customer satisfaction because consumers typically do not know who mined their gemstone or metal. But for a car or appliance maker, reputation can bleed into satisfaction measures, and marketing and sales data can help identify the costs of that. How, for example, does a company's philanthropy or HR policy affect customer perceptions?

Analyzed this way, initiatives that might otherwise be classified as costs can become drivers of revenue. Without this sort of analysis, the costs of sourcing from the cheapest garment factories in Bangladesh, or of high employee turnover, may not be factored into strategic decision-making. To do this analysis, you must collect measurable, verifiable information on customer preferences *and* how they are affected by activities such as philanthropy. You cannot assume a connection.

Similarly, decisions made by the marketing and sales and HR departments may impact suppliers' views of a company. Suppliers may wish to be associated with firms that adhere to best practices with respect to employees or the environment. They may see a benefit of such an association in dealings with *their* stakeholders. Or they may wish to learn about these practices in the belief that collaboration could lead to opportunities. Either way, suppliers may be willing to offer better terms or provide other benefits. Identifying and quantifying these benefits requires collaboration with purchasing staffers. They may know that a particular supplier offered better terms because it wanted to work with your firm. But that information might not have been fed into overall budgeting and planning.

Turning next to employees, productivity, turnover and recruitment costs should be calculated too. A large body of scholarship also highlights the impact on employees of creating and activating closer connections to downstream customers who benefit from the firm's products or services. Supply chain practices and engagement with broader social issues could have a similar impact, particularly in highly competitive job markets. People want to work with firms that are recognized as exemplars of best practice.

The most difficult to measure, but arguably the most important, benefits and costs stem from new business development. How do potential customers, suppliers and employees as well as external stakeholders such as government officials and representatives of civil society perceive the firm? Which actions can managers take today to ensure more rapid permitting, access, support, attention and effort? How might you credibly quantify these?

Estimating data

Ideally, internal numbers could answer all of these questions, but often no such numbers exist and they cannot easily be gathered. Collection thus requires a great deal of estimation of the financial and operational returns to corporate diplomacy. Those estimates should draw upon not just internal information but also the public reports of peer firms and analyses by respected industry associations, policymakers and academics. For example, when estimating the potential cost of regulatory fines or legal judgments, one can survey government documents to ascertain the frequency, amount and distribution of such costs across firms of various types.

Where data is not available, subjectivity plays a role. Avoid the delegation of subjective judgments to staffers who have a direct interest in a given strategic choice. For example, when seeking to identify the employee retention impact of a sustainability initiative, assessment must come from HR personnel, not sustainability staffers. And all the data should be validated and approved by financial managers. Without such safeguards, estimates will run into accusations of bias.

In a recent workshop I conducted, one sustainability specialist estimated that worker productivity would increase 20% if a company invested more in engagement. The reasoning? Workers would spend less time criticizing or undermining operations and more time supporting them. Maybe this is true, but it is too aggressive to assume so without input from HR.

While this process of allocation of responsibility is easy to articulate, it is typically far more difficult to implement. Time constraints, initiative fatigue and overlapping reporting requirements often overwhelm managers who sometimes feel that they have no time to do their actual jobs. Yet another corporate initiative with ever-more meetings and reporting requirements can frequently be met with a closed door or unreturned phone calls.

Overcoming this hurdle requires its own internal engagement strategy. Senior management buy-in is critical. A champion's support can help to ward off accusations of bias. What is more, the champion can show how engagement connects to other corporate goals. Otherwise, it might be dismissed by colleagues as time wasted.

The first role of the champion should be assembling an interdepartmental team. Team members should include people from corporate diplomacy (i.e., governmental affairs, external affairs, legal, communications, community and sustainability), but also operations and logistics, design or R&D, environment and health, marketing, and finance and accounting, among others. Ideally, the work of quantifying corporate diplomacy programs by this team will begin with a meeting in which a few key diplomacy initiatives or stakeholder-related risks are identified. This meeting should focus on initiatives with the greatest potential to save money or increase revenue. Participants should brainstorm about the scope of potential impacts on cash flow. According to an internal analysis by the IFC of projects that they have funded, risks to consider include:

- The potential for legal action (i.e., number of lawsuits or financial penalties per year, length of operational delays that these cause and the associated costs)

- Delays to planning, construction or operations (i.e., number of disruptions per year, the duration of those disruptions and associated costs)

- Project expropriation (i.e., probability of the nationalization of a facility)

In the case of Newmont's Ahafo mine, the team focused on only the following indirect impacts, which team members believed they could measure with precision:

- **Fewer roadblocks and production interruptions.** Before the engagement campaign, interruptions occurred about every other year. These lasted, on average, one week and cost about $3 million. No incidents had occurred since 2003

- **Fewer complaints.** Before engagement, local people filed an average of 12 serious complaints a year to Newmont, which led to investigative and follow-up costs of about $50,000 per complaint

- **Fewer protests.** Before engagement, protests would suspend exploration roughly every other year at a cost of approximately $5 million per suspension

- **Fewer fines and legal judgments.** Early on, legal problems arose about every three years at a cost of $3 million for each case

- **Fewer protests about water availability and quality.** Water complaints had previously occurred every other year, generating approximately $200,000 in remediation costs each time

At the end of the kick-off session, a project leader should be identified to oversee the estimation process. Ideally, this person would be an accountant or finance professional with a reputation for fairness and an ability to dig up data that may not be easy to extract. Over the coming weeks, he or she will validate the speculative analysis presented at the workshop and spend time with representatives from each department discussing costs and lost revenues and pulling together best estimates from current operations, historical data and peers. This person must record the assumptions behind their calculations. Inevitably, the analysis will be challenged by peers. Any mistakes or unrealistic assumptions could undermine the credibility of the entire process.

The data gathered should be used in the DCF analysis of current and potential corporate diplomacy initiatives. That analysis can be conducted by using a firm's own techniques or by using the FVTOOL developed by the IFC, the Norwegian Ministry of Foreign Affairs and Deloitte.

Given the probabilistic nature of much of the analysis, it is important to present not only the expected value of the corporate diplomacy initiatives but also the distribution of that value *and* its sensitivity to the assumptions. The expected value of an initiative should not be the only outcome measure. Instead, that value should be presented with the percentage of cases in which that expected value is above various thresholds and the sensitivity of these estimates to the assumptions. Where a single assumption regarding the probability or one-time cost of an event has a disproportionate impact on the calculations, those assumptions or estimates should be subject to correspondingly large scrutiny.

An important outcome of this process is the transformation of the dialogue around corporate diplomacy. Quantifying financial benefits helps to show how intelligent measurement and tracking can improve the effectiveness of engagement and how the benefits of diplomacy flow to the bottom line. This can transform the dialogue about corporate diplomacy from one in which skeptics demand a justification for current costs to one in which they work with corporate diplomats to jointly identify new opportunities to create value. Showing colleagues that corporate diplomacy can create financial value can turn these skeptics into evangelists, who return to their departments and lobby on behalf of stakeholder engagement.

Diplomats' Talking Points and Checklist

Corporate diplomats seeking to build support for the adoption of this approach can point to Newmont Ahafo. The benefits there of NPV calculations went beyond finding a high return on investment from engagement. The exercise also changed the way that sustainability team members went about their jobs. Early on, some of them had questioned the morality of calculating the NPV of their work. But afterwards, they championed the FVTOOL. On top of this, their status within the company had risen as they were seen as more professional and essential. Having learned the language of finance, they could better communicate with colleagues. Staffers from other departments, likewise, could see how sustainability contributed to financial and operational performance, and better understood its contribution to overall corporate goals. In the words of two interviewees from the ESR team that I interviewed as part of my research on Newmont Ahafo:

> When we first heard of it, those of us on the social side were happy to get something that would help finance understand us. We are more confident in costing the programs that we do. This puts us in a much better position with finance. In previous meetings, other departments had figures, and we had to talk to explain. Now we are putting figures to our words just like other departments.

> The change within the ESR team is marked. What are these risks that we are trying to mitigate? Are their costs justified in terms of risk mitigation? Previously, program owners were not connecting the dots to risk mitigation or value creation. Now we challenge the numbers. Previously, we had no framework to evaluate. People are now trying to highlight the value of their initiatives for the business not just for stakeholders.

An interviewee from the finance department concurred:

> My biggest surprise was that it is possible for the ESR team to have a conversation on financial terms. Every conversation I had with them before ... [t]hey could never articulate their assumptions and acknowledge costs and benefits. Now they can and do ... They have their act together and can explain a business case ... Previously, they were not able to see their business case ... finance and

[environment and social responsibility] are now working together much better than before. Just those changes alone justify the effort put into the pilot.

Another finance professional reinforced this sense of progress:

In the last business-planning meeting, I saw a huge improvement in SR's presentation of their budget, which was supported by data of the business benefits of SR programs. The meeting went very smoothly compared to previous meetings.

Sustainability staffers saw their work acknowledged outside of Ghana, too, since their bosses had begun using it to justify Newmont's commitment to sustainability during presentations to shareholders and financial analysts. They cited the acceleration of the land acquisition, productivity gains in their workforce and savings from investing in water and sanitation infrastructure. In fact, all of the teams that met to share data and discuss the NPV calculations left with a new appreciation for the many ways that the company impacted external stakeholders.

Sustainability was no longer seen as money wasted. Senior management recognized that there was a strategic reason to fund these programs. This change in attitude has not happened only at Ahafo but also at other FVTOOL early adopters, including several other major mining companies. Consultancies such as Deloitte and others were promoting the tool in multiple industries, including oil and gas, forestry, agribusiness and even heavy manufacturing. The experiences at Ahafo had even found their way into the required curriculum of leading business schools and industry training schemes. Practitioners had long sensed the business justification for corporate citizenship and community goodwill, but quantifying the value proved those benefits to others. In a phrase coined by Newmont's executive for environmental and social responsibility, quantifying the NPV of sustainability initiatives at Ahafo Ghana had finally allowed the company to get "beyond net present value."

Corporate diplomacy will always be both science and art. It will always require both counting and listening, quantifying and empathizing. At some level, it is the difficult pairing of a tough mind and a soft heart that drives successful engagement.

Had AES had access to these tools in Georgia, its managers might have concluded, as did the only other bidder for the asset, Électricité de France, that the appropriate bid price was much lower. They might have seen the importance of a financial partnership with the US and European Union sooner. They also might have worked harder and earlier to identify a reliable and politically powerful independent source of fuel. The only viable option would seem to be the coalition of BP and the Italian firm ENI who were building the Bakhu-Tbilisi-Ceyhan pipeline to transport Azerbaijani oil and gas to Turkey and Europe. It is questionable whether BP and ENI would have wanted to form such a deal given the implications it would have for their own relations with Russia. Finally, when confronted with Russian opposition, they might have had better information to inform the choice to either continue Scholey's strategy with external financial assistance or, if financial neutrality was truly required, sell out earlier to the Russians.

If you seek to deploy NPV calculations in your company in support of corporate diplomacy initiatives, be sure to:

- Familiarize yourself and your team with the core business systems and processes of the other functional areas of the organization

- Convene a cross-functional team to manage data collection and analysis and appoint as leader of that team someone from the most respected or powerful department

- Identify three to ten initiatives to be modeled and two to five scenarios (i.e., options) within each area

- For each scenario identify

  – Direct costs and revenue gains

  – Indirect costs and revenue gains

» Draw upon your risk registry to identify baseline stake-holder-related risks

» Update your risk registry if necessary

» Consider which scenarios and initiatives are most likely to increase social license

» Brainstorm about the likelihood that these ranked scenarios and initiatives will alter the probabilities of the risks occurring and their impact. These estimates should be probabilistic

Three

Personal:

Stakeholder relationships are personal relationships

The implementation of stakeholder engagement has received much attention from practitioners and academics. Scads of frameworks have been offered—their numerousness and variety can overwhelm. The most cited, and most commonly found on the desks of practitioners, is *Getting it Right* by Luc Zandvliet and Mary B. Anderson, but other related texts include *Corporate-Community Involvement* by Nick Larkin and Veronica Scheubel, *Corporate Social Responsibility* by Philip Kotler and Nancy Lee, and *Capitalism at the Crossroads* by Stuart Hart.

Many of these books boil down to the same simple message: companies, governments and NGOs, in dealing with stakeholders, should set aside self-interested calculations of efficiency in favor of something like the Golden Rule—do unto others as you would have them do unto you. Each author then offers his or her own system for achieving this lofty goal. What I offer here is both a synthesis of these findings and a structure through which to implement them.

Recall that the goal of corporate diplomacy is to enhance financial and operational performance by improving the degree to which stakeholders grant your firm the social license to operate. Robert Boutilier, one of the scholars who has done the most to operational-ize the idea of the social license,[108] talks about the concept not as a single threshold to be crossed but as something like a pyramid to be climbed, with each level building on the previous level.

The pyramid's base is economic legitimacy—the feeling among stakeholders that a company offers a net economic benefit to them. The next levels are interactional trust—that a company listens and keeps promises—and sociopolitical legitimacy—that the company respects culture and customs and acts fairly. At the apex of the pyra-mid is what Boutilier calls institutionalized trust—the sense that the company has an enduring regard for stakeholder interests. Here, the barrier between the company and stakeholders dissipates, and each side demonstrates an enduring regard for the interests of the other. Either is willing to give to the other because they no longer perceive the other as an opponent; rather, they see each other as allies. What can your firm do to achieve institutionalized trust?

My answer is rooted not in economics but partly in the study of public housing in the US. One framework on which I draw was devel-oped by Sherry Arnstein, an official in the US Department of Housing and Urban Development. In 1969, Arnstein published an article,[109] which has become a classic among scholars, laying out what she called the "ladder of public participation." Her objective was to show the spectrum of possible involvement by have-nots in any political proc-ess. She distinguished empty rituals of participation, mainly designed to dupe stakeholders into thinking they had a voice, from real partici-patory power. She stressed that the most popular means of interacting with stakeholders are often little more than scams, intended not to build trust and support but only to create the appearance of it.

At the bottom of Arnstein's ladder is "manipulation," where, she wrote: '[Stakeholders] "are placed on rubberstamp advisory com-mittees for the express purpose of 'educating' them." Or, even more cynically, to show the broader public that they have input. Her next rung was "therapy." Here, education is intended to shift the opinions of residents to bring them into line with the interests of government officials and to distract them from their real concerns. One rung higher is "informing" through one-way communication, including use of media, pamphlets, posters and responses to queries or complaints. This entails talking but not listening. It is like an old-school ad campaign, where the audience is bombarded with messages.

The rung above that, "consultation," moves to two-way communication. It consists of surveys, neighborhood meetings and public hearings in which a government agency solicits the views of the stakeholders but, critically, cedes no authority. Arnstein was dismissive of this, too: "When powerholders restrict the input of citizens' ideas solely to this level, participation remains just a window-dressing ritual."

Formal authority begins to be ceded to stakeholders—and real participation begins—with "placation." Here, a few stakeholder representatives, deemed worthy by the government agency, receive seats on boards with real power. But, Arnstein wrote, if these appointees "are not accountable to a constituency in the community and if the traditional power elite hold the majority of seats, the have-nots can be easily outvoted and outfoxed."

Arnstein's highest three rungs begin with "partnership," which represents genuine power sharing between the government and residents. Next comes "delegated power," where the government cedes to residents decision-making authority over a particular project or program. The final and highest rung is "citizen control," where residents are given the authority and resources to succeed. Examples of citizen control include local cooperatives in the utility, agriculture or small-scale manufacturing sectors.

Substitute "investor" for "government official" and "stakeholder" for "resident," and Arnstein's ladder can apply to corporate stakeholder engagement. Ideally, multinationals, having assessed stakeholder preferences and power structures, would seek to cede control to communities and provide them with the resources necessary to meet their objectives. In reality, companies often do not climb Arnstein's ladder, preferring instead to opt for the appearance of engagement provided by its lower rungs.

That is unfortunate because even the top rungs of Arnstein's ladder fall short of the best practices of corporate diplomacy on at least two counts. First, she ignored whether stakeholders had the resources to meet their goals. Stakeholders, particularly in the developing world, are often poor and uneducated. Even if a company wants to cede control to them, they may not have the wherewithal to assume it. They may need help—money and expertise. What is more, a company is typically entering a situation where the government has done a bad job providing public goods and, as a result, is resented and distrusted. In that situation, a critical consideration is whether a multinational should provide the necessary resources directly. Even a weak or corrupt government is likely to have some infrastructure for assistance. Yet its bad reputation could undermine, even poison, attempts at engagement.

Consider the bedevilments facing oil companies operating in the Ogoni Delta in Nigeria. The region is rife with conflict. There is the conflict between local communities, political organizations and paramilitary groups and national political and military authorities over the distribution of economic resources and political power. Investors in Bolivia similarly face conflict between the relatively poor and historically less politically powerful indigenous population of the northern and western highlands and the relatively wealthier, more urban and immigrant lowland population. A more complete framework must consider the extent to which the multinational faced with such pre-existing conflicts should step in to provide the necessary economic resources either indirectly (i.e., through the government) or directly, and what is the limit for such contributions.

A broader engagement framework than Arnstein's also must consider the possibility that some stakeholders will not agree, not because of a lack of capacity but because it is in their interest not to. Maybe their objectives conflict with those of other stakeholders. Or maybe they benefit from the status quo or even from continued conflict. An example that crops up in conflicts around the world are poorly educated youth who lack skills other than bullying and quasi-military coercion. These people may fear the loss of status and power that peace would bring and thus might seek to foment continued conflict.

The more common framework for thinking about stakeholder engagement is offered by Luc Zandvliet and Mary B. Anderson in their 2009 book *Getting it Right: Making Corporate-Community Relations Work*. They focus on four principles divided across two domains, which can apply to hiring, compensation, contracting, community consultation and community projects, as well as collaboration with NGOs and governments. Their principles are fairness and transparency in the distribution of benefits, and respect, care and transparency in corporate behavior (i.e., actions of employees). Benefits should be distributed and costs allocated in a manner that is perceived as fair according to local norms, that rewards long-term cooperation and that penalizes self-serving behavior and violence. Zandvliet and Anderson argue that engagement should be as transparent and clearly communicated as possible to encourage input from stakeholders. Corporate actions should demonstrate respect, trust and caring, and should avoid reinforcement of a sense of distance between company employees and community members. But they, too, sidestep the question of the sufficiency and origin of economic resources and, to a lesser extent, the problem of managing existing conflict. Furthermore, their text, while providing guidance across a wide array of contexts, offers more of a generalist set of principles than a structured set of tools and approaches as offered by Arnstein or that which follows here.

Eroding or undermining the social license

Conflict is linked to the most damaging form of stakeholder engagement: coercion, typically supported by the threat of physical violence by an ally such as the military, a local warlord, or gangs. In response to threats or violence, opposition may crumble; opponents may go silent or leave.

A classic example of coercion—and how it can backfire—is the role of United Fruit Company in the toppling of the democratically elected government of Jacobo Arbenz in Guatemala in 1954. President Arbenz had threatened to implement land reform, which United Fruit perceived as unfavorable to its interests. Working with CIA operative Howard Hunt, who had later become infamous as one of the architects of the Watergate burglary in the US, the company funded a paramilitary group led by an exiled former army officer named Carlos Armas. Armas's invasion force was tiny—480 soldiers—but the expectation that it would receive support from US naval and marine forces led to a mass defection of Guatemalan soldiers to Armas's insurgency and also to Arbenz's resignation. Tactically, United Fruit won but, in so doing, it discredited itself with most of the people of Guatemala. Armas himself would be the victim of a coup in 1960, and Guatemala would plunge into a 36-year civil war that would destroy the holdings that United Fruit had sought so desperately to protect.

Less damaging and dangerous, but still a failure, is a tick-box approach to engagement. Here, companies report compliance with the Equator Principles,[110] or some other recognized criteria, and issue annual reports full of glossy photos of smiling stakeholders. Those efforts amount to little more than propaganda. Checklists and photos often mask a situation where compliant or powerless stakeholders were included for their value as "poster people" but given no real voice. One mining company operating in a poor central African nation, for example, touted its annual stakeholder consultation, but an outside review found that, after much fanfare at launch and the collection of numerous grievances, there was no follow-up. Each subsequent annual meeting was attended by fewer and less senior stakeholders who raised the same longstanding grievances and continued to report no follow-up. They perceived the company as wasting their time and not heeding their concerns.

A more involved form of interaction, but one that still fails to build the social license, is therapy. Here, the investor devotes time and resources to communicating why it cannot meet its commitments or how it is not responsible for grievances. Company representatives will even shift the blame onto the stakeholders, highlighting how they have contributed to their own plight. They will say things such as: "If only so many migrants hadn't arrived in search of employment opportunities, the water supply would not have been overwhelmed"; "If only farmers had diversified their crops and used better practices, they wouldn't be facing such low prices". Excuses, even where valid, patronize and demean. They presume that an outsider can assess the causes of stakeholder grievances without understanding of the local context. They are perceived as efforts to lecture rather than listen, to evade rather than engage.

The foundation of social license

The foundation for the social license to operate is a sense that stakeholders are better off thanks to the presence of the investor. Surprisingly, investors often assume that this is true—their usual argument is that they are creating jobs and improving infrastructure. They also assume that stakeholders share their view. But a smart diplomat does not assume. He or she has the data at hand to highlight a firm's total economic contribution in a transparent and comprehensible manner. At the very least, she or he provides data demonstrating the distribution of new jobs and contracts within a community, region or country. Other contributions that might be highlighted include the percentage of exports, foreign direct investment and gross domestic output. Data also might extend to information on the royalties and taxes paid and even the spillover benefits of these direct payments.

Expenditures related to corporate social responsibility, such as payments to meet political or social objectives, are pertinent too. Here, both inputs—financial and in-kind contributions—and outputs—social or economic indicators—should be offered. The sorts of information provided might include the following.

- Payments for worker training, information on hours of training provided and evidence of productivity gains or improvements in employment prospects

- Increased capacity for local firms. This might include assistance with qualification for tenders, worker and management training, access to finance and technology and new business opportunities. Typical indicators are the number of firms that received assistance and evidence of gains in revenue, employment or profitability

- Community development grants and infrastructure improvements such as water, electricity, sanitation, education, transportation and healthcare. Metrics might include the number of people served or illnesses treated or prevented

- Environmental remediation. Evidence here comes in the form of tests of water and air quality and proof of waste reduction

This sort of presentation of facts can help build a foundation of understanding and trust between the firm and external stakeholders. But facts alone will not win social license. Persuasion and education, earnestly offered, matter too.

In one exchange relayed to me, a prominent government official challenged the managing director of a foreign operation regarding his company's contribution to the local economy. The official complained of the profits that the company made in the country, and claimed that less than 0.1% of them were being re-invested there. The managing director was taken aback. The number cited was not profits but revenue. Furthermore, the cited funds spent on development included only a legally mandated contribution to a social fund and none of the measurable economic benefits of the company's presence.

This exchange triggered a lengthy discussion of the firm's costs, which included substantial tax and royalty payments to the government, as well as payments to national contractors and employees. While relations did not immediately shift from acrimonious to amicable, the executive's ability to address misconceptions in a genial way at least created a basis for further dialogue.

Interactional trust

Stakeholders vary in their location, education, language, literacy and confidence in different sources of information. Efforts to communicate with them must account for this variety. The first step in developing the social license is, to paraphrase George Bernard Shaw, overcoming the illusion that communication has taken place.

An information campaign should include not only media buys but also signage near the investor's operations and, when appropriate, in village squares and markets. Signs should include pictures and easy-to-understand graphics, and the use of simple language. And communication cannot just be left to the media. People must participate: executives should meet stakeholders face to face. These meetings should be arranged not only with the mighty—government grandees, bankers and the like—but also with the meek—labor representatives, community activists and average folk who have an interest in a project.

Meetings like these will help a firm move from force-feeding its information to stakeholders to consulting them and trying to understand their priorities. (Such efforts are at the core of the due diligence described in Chapter 2.) In meetings, company representatives must not only probe for stakeholder concerns but should seek to build trust. By listening and sharing their own experiences, they will gain a more nuanced understanding of stakeholders' preferences. This understanding can help them identify points of similarity (e.g., we both have teenage daughters or play pick-up soccer) that can help overcome perceptions of distance and hierarchy, or the feeling that a relationship is purely mercantile. In the beginning, low-cost gestures of understanding and empathy are powerful means to forge deeper relationships. To ensure that the process progresses, gestures should be reciprocated, questions and concerns addressed and commitments met. Failure to do so will reinforce distrust and beliefs that an investor sees itself as superior or detached.

Occasionally, it may be useful to convene larger groups of stakeholders for dialogue and decision-making. Multi-stakeholder meetings can work, but they must be carefully choreographed, or else some participants can feel manipulated when more powerful peers outvote them. All of the stakeholders present must have a common goal. And they must be able to interact peaceably; the danger of fisticuffs, or worse, precludes the possibility of productive dialogue. A respected facilitator should be agreed upon and that person should know the situation and the stakeholders. Typically, facilitators come from the non-profit sector but are willing and eager to forge partnerships with multinationals. While straightforward in concept, this process can take months or years to execute. All too often, senior managers see a consultative meeting as a one-off event that will give rise to a grand compromise which lets them "get on with it." Such unrealistic time pressure can undermine even the best-designed process, again leaving the stakeholders to perceive it as no more than manipulation.

A successful example of consultation can be found at the Tintaya copper mine in Peru.[111] There, BHP Billiton overcame stakeholder resentment against the government and prior mine owners and operators by engaging in a multi-year dialogue. Following the principles outlined above, BHP identified a facilitator in Antonio Bernales, an independent Lima-based consultant and founder of Futuro Sostenible, a Peruvian non-profit. He worked to bring stakeholders to the common understanding that they both wanted the mine to succeed in a manner that benefited the community. He then elicited their key concerns, which included human rights, economic development, pollution and land compensation. On each issue, he convened a task force of volunteers, which worked to craft an action plan acceptable to all. This seemingly simple process required almost two years of regular meetings before proposals were offered to the BHP about how best to proceed. Meantime, there was much recrimination about the proclivity to talk instead of do and even accusations that the company was stalling.

One critical element in building and maintaining interactional trust is managing the expectations of stakeholders. A sure way to corrode a relationship is to fail to reciprocate, respond or meet initial commitments. Such failures quickly lead to a reputation as untrustworthy, even manipulative. This is of particular concern when the managers who do the early negotiations differ from those tasked with construction or operations. The temptation for the negotiators to overcommit without considering the cost in terms of long-term stakeholder dissatisfaction is overwhelming. Even in the absence of this challenge, managers must be aware of the expectations that their words and actions are creating. Explaining what a firm cannot do, and how it decides that, may be as important, or even more important, than offering advice and assistance.

Another key factor is understanding and managing emotions. People tend to be xenophobic, trusting people similar to them more than they trust those who are different. They stereotype too, letting their emotions, not objective analysis, influence how they respond. To what extent can representatives of your company recognize the emotional state of stakeholders from non-verbal cues? How good are they at managing and conveying emotions to stakeholders in a manner that reinforces, rather than undermines, trust? In any interaction with stakeholders, managers need to keep in mind not only what is being said and done but also felt. Do they project positive affect? Do stakeholders have a sense that managers are happy to be there or that they are there out of obligation and eager to return to other activities?

BHP may have been successful in Tintaya because Lucio Rios, the deputy manager at the site, took part in an executive training program on sustainability and community impact in Orissa, India.

A co-participant claimed that the experience changed Rios. "We saw communities. How poor! We saw the other side of the road. We put ourselves in the community's shoes. We lived in tents, and there was a lack of water to wash ourselves." Paul Warner, a BHP executive who worked closely with Rios, reported that: "He went on this trip and it was like Saul on the road to Damascus ... He saw the light and he was under a lot of pressure to see the light, but he came back from India a changed man. Everything he did after that was like night and day." Rios himself said: "In India, I spent time with people who had lost their lands and who had suffered immensely as a result of the construction of a massive hydroelectric dam. Having seen what they went through, I was forced to ask myself if my own actions had led to something very similar at Tintaya." After this transformative experience, Rios's interactions with stakeholders were characterized by greater empathy and understanding as well as a genuine desire to improve stakeholders' lives. According to staff from NGOs that participated in the process, these personal and emotional factors helped to convince skeptics that BHP-Billiton was serious about reform.

Sociopolitical legitimacy

Good manners and emotional intelligence matter, but so do international norms about human rights and local norms about social interactions. In interactions with stakeholders, managers must be sensitive to both. They should show respect for local traditions and beliefs. However, where local norms conflict with their global ones on, for example, the inclusion of women, minority groups or outcasts, managers must err on the side of inclusion without patronizing. Similarly, the outcomes of their interactions must be perceived as fair and appropriate by both local and global stakeholders.

Timing matters too. Stakeholder engagement should start as early as possible in the life of a project or the employment of a manager. Reaching out early demonstrates respect and highlights a foreign firm's recognition of its status as a guest. Waiting until there is a formal public approval or, worse, a public outcry, reinforces distrust. The difference between seeking social license and defending officially granted permits can be the difference between success and failure in international projects.

Introductions in early meetings are also critically important. Who is the first known stakeholder with whom you are seen? Who introduces you? Where do these meetings take place? Do you follow local norms in terms of gifts and good manners? In which order do you visit other stakeholders? Which stakeholders do you fail to reach out to or treat as lower status? Knowing little, if anything, about you, stakeholders will infer a great deal from these initial actions. Consider the contrast between stakeholders first learning about a potential investment project when a private jet arrives carrying a CEO who emerges to shake hands with a local gangster and is then spirited in a limo to the mayor's office and the impression left when the same CEO is walked through the community by a respected local leader who introduces the CEO to all the leader's friends on the way to their joint meeting with the mayor.

Similarly, commitment to stakeholder interactions can reinforce or undermine a well-designed and executed introduction. How frequent are consultations? Where do they happen? Does one side dictate the timing of the meetings? Who participates from the company? Do the company's representatives demonstrate a clear commitment to deepening the relationship or do their efforts seem perfunctory? Do representatives from the company attend important local events and act like gracious guests? Attendance at some local ceremonies may seem tedious—just as, for example, ribbon cuttings are at home—but, if stakeholders see them as important, managers should show respect by participating. Beyond formal opportunities for interaction, how frequent are ad hoc meetings? Are representatives of the company fenced off in a secured compound (which, granted, is occasionally necessary), or are they part of the community?

While there is no universal definition of fairness, it is important to consider whether outcomes unduly reward privileged stakeholders.

Any sense that outcomes, however arrived at, benefit such people will likely lead to perceptions of unfairness and a loss of the social license. A question always worth asking of any outcome is: "How would this play on YouTube?" In today's Internet-connected world, that is where anything that you do not want the public to see will end up.

Another pitfall is the appearance of favoring corrupt insiders or bullies. Such outcomes can rapidly set off vicious cycles in which some stakeholders compete to be the biggest bully, undermining the broader effort at consultation and trust building. Corporate diplomacy should highlight and reward behavior that solves problems peaceably and spans social boundaries.

Regardless of the perceived fairness of the outcome, the process of decision-making also influences stakeholder opinions. Where an outcome was arrived at through an inclusive process, stakeholders will be more accepting than where it was arrived at via back-room dealings. Thus, corporate diplomats should share information with stakeholders regarding their respective contributions and likely returns. They should provide a safe environment for stakeholders to share their opinions. They should also ensure that stakeholders perceive their solicitations of input as genuine. Any sense that the process patronizes will undermine trust.

Managers also must respond to feedback in a way that treats everyone fairly. Your answer to a request may be 'No,' but the process of arriving at that answer, and the standard for treating one stakeholder differently from another, must be clearly communicated and consistently applied. This final element is among the most critical and difficult to implement. A clear explanation of which demands and claims managers cannot address, and why, is a key component of corporate diplomacy.

Acquiring sociopolitical legitimacy requires an understanding of a locale's tacit social rules. What are stakeholder expectations around meetings, gifts, small-talk and other social conventions? How acceptable is confrontation, and how much do personal and professional lives overlap? What are norms regarding punctuality, attire, discussion of religion and politics, personal space, direct eye contact, posture, physical contact and the tolerance for inequity? Do managers understand and appreciate the history of the area, local traditions and beliefs? Most important, are they able not only to recognize differences but also to bridge them to forge stronger interpersonal relationships?

A good example of the importance of sociopolitical legitimacy is the prominent role played by respect for local culture and tradition, including dancing, in the multi-stakeholder dialogue table at the Ambuklao-Binga hydroelectric dam in the Philippines.[112] The original stakeholder complaints stretched from resettlement to economic opportunities. But through dialogue, the focus of engagement shifted to long-standing grievances by indigenous people who felt that the national government and the elite more broadly did not value them and their cultural traditions. Thus, the decision by the government and private investors to cede authority over a wide swath of land around the dam to indigenous people for the development of a cultural heritage site was critical in securing support and building trust.

A partnership approach

To achieve institutionalized trust, engagement professionals must remove the distinction between "us" and "them." They must convince local stakeholders that they share an enduring interest in the same long-term objectives. They must share, delegate or even cede power over the issues most important to stakeholders and invite stakeholders to participate in the monitoring and evaluation of the firm's commitments and actions. They must enable stakeholders to address their most pressing problems. Often capacity building requires the formation and support for multi-stakeholder partnerships, with the assistance of NGOs and governments. Such an approach may be more costly or time consuming than addressing the symptoms of those problems but, ultimately, capacity building pays off in terms of building social license.

Efforts to achieve cooperation among stakeholders have been branded a partnership approach. While there is no single formula for a successful partnership, key elements include repeated multi-stakeholder workshops that result in a "partnership agreement" early on and frequent follow-up meetings, clear agreement about objectives and regular monitoring of their achievement, creation of a means of dispute resolution, and buy-in from participants, including top management. Frank upfront discussion of what constitutes fair dealing helps to create norms that guide behavior.

More recently, scholars have emphasized the use of sophisticated shared simulations to allow group visualization and joint evaluation of project outcomes for different scenarios and networked communications among project team members, to facilitate interparty negotiations and foster shared identity.

An example of such an effort is the Newmont Ahafo Development Foundation (NADeF) in Ghana, near Newmont's Ahafo gold mine.[113] Newmont annually contributes $1 per ounce of gold produced and 1% of Ahafo's net profit to the foundation. Modeled on Newmont's experience in Peru, NADeF made grants to local projects that were likely to be sustainable and that reflected the interests of the community. Community members and Newmont representatives jointly govern NADeF. The foundation seeks to involve contractors and other members of the value chain in its operations, both through voluntary donations and in-kind contributions. Each community also forms a sustainable development committee with members from youth groups, women's groups, unit committees, traditional authorities (e.g., religious leaders or tribal chiefs) and other community members.

Funds are allocated among member communities with a weighting system that gives more money to communities that are more severely impacted by the mine, demonstrate a greater commitment to the foundation, have more people and have more land area in the mining lease.

Within each community, the foundation seeks to allocate its funds so that 24% go to human resource development (e.g., scholarships and job training), 23% to infrastructure (e.g., water, electricity, roads, clinics/health centers, schools, toilet facilities and incinerators), 18% to social amenities (e.g., community centers, police posts and libraries), 17% to economic empowerment (e.g., employment, entrepreneurship, credit and capacity building), 12% to natural resource protection, and 6% to cultural heritage and sports. To date, over 2,000 students have received scholarships and 30 projects have been completed, including the construction of teachers' quarters (to house teachers who had previously commuted up to 50 kilometers), new classrooms, libraries, and mechanized boreholes to provide access to underground water, electrification, public toilets and medical clinics. Newmont managers believed the fund to be among their most important legacies in Ghana.

Ceding of control in this way often causes consternation among investors. Does it really make sense to devote corporate resources to a process that the company does not control? Isn't there a risk of corruption? These risks are real, and managers must help stakeholders craft evaluation and monitoring criteria that minimize them without appearing to patronize or condescend. Capacity building of stakeholders with a particular emphasis on local public sector and civil society groups is often a precursor to negotiations with them on a strategy to address their needs. Despite the financial costs and time involved, there is no initiative with a greater return in terms of removing the divide between a firm and stakeholders than one that equips stakeholders with the ability to address their most pressing concerns.

Symbols and rituals help in persuading stakeholders to support efforts like this. It may be possible to win stakeholders support through the use of unified imagery (e.g., logos, terminology or other branding campaigns), stories, rituals or symbolic actions (e.g., associations with charities or causes). These techniques forge a shared identity. The shared development and wide distribution of a project logo or stakeholder and management participation in football leagues, for example, may serve to overcome identity barriers and increase the likelihood of cooperation.

A prominent example here comes from the pro bono consulting opportunities offered in recent years by McKinsey, Accenture and other multinationals. Employees of these firms compete for assignments to do non-profit consulting in challenging domestic or international locations, often in collaboration with NGOs or government agencies. These assignments provide little or no revenue to the parent. Sometimes, innovations and information filter back, but the larger benefits come from the effect on employees. They are typically recharged and inspired by the impact that they make. These initiatives do present the risk that good employees will be so affected by the experience that they leave the parent firm. To minimize this risk, companies try to link their corporate identity to the assignment and, on return from the assignment, ensure that employees feel that their experiences are valued by colleagues.

Frequently, the legitimate needs and concerns of stakeholders overwhelm an investor's capacity to assist. Despite high potential returns, the required investments do not allow sufficient surplus to satisfy stakeholder demands. Even in cases where investors possess sufficient capital, they may not want to set into motion a dynamic where they are perceived to be writing blank checks. Escalating demands, and overly optimistic expectations, can make investors regret their initial generosity. Providing resources may delay or even undermine stakeholders' willingness to address their needs themselves.

For all these reasons, the goal of any initiative should be, where possible, to develop local capacity to address problems. Efforts to appropriately set expectations, explain what the investor can and cannot do, and share information, can help stem the replication of failed corporate engagement efforts that produced only unstaffed schools, unstocked dispensaries and overflowing latrines—and, of course, resentment. Investors may provide seed capital and resources and connect stakeholders to NGOs, government agencies and other potential contributors and collaborators, but, ultimately the only sustainable engagement strategy is one that stakeholders want and nurture for themselves.

Diplomats' talking points and checklist

Corporate diplomats seeking to build support for the adoption of this approach can point to the case of Chevron in Nigeria[114] and the transformation in its communities' program after a spasm of violence in 2003, which forced an 18-month shutdown of its operations. Dennis Flemming who was Chevron's representative to the Niger Delta Partnership Initiative, explained: "You know the mindset was, you know, let's do something for the community, we can sit around a conference table. We can figure out what we want to do for them, and then we go out and deliver these benefits, this largesse for the communities." Local stakeholders understood that Chevron was not really listening. Reverend Dr IC Tolar of the Egbema-Gbaramato Regional Development Council Warri said: "They came to our communities with their packed lunch and drinks . . . and said we can do these projects for you." Edmund Tiemo of the Egbema-Gbaramato Community Development Foundation said: "Chevron operated a cash-handout system for the community leaders . . . What they were doing was just appeasing community leaders. That's what Chevron was doing. But, they didn't listen." Professor Femi Ajibola of the NGO New Nigeria Foundation elaborated: "There are many companies that are well-intentioned but they don't understand the process of development. So they think, 'Oh, they need schools. They need hospitals. We can do that. . . . We can build them a school. We can build them a hospital.' The unfortunate thing is that, number one, you cannot sit down and decide the needs and requirements of others for them. Number two, you cannot prioritize for them. Number three, even if you get it right—that is, you are able to identify what they need—it is extremely important that they own the process and that they own the structures in place for their development."

During the 2003–2004 conflict, the hospitals and schools that Chevron had previously built had been burned or destroyed. Professor Ajibola explains that the hospitals and schools "were

→

never thought of being owned by the community from day one. They always thought it was owned by the person that did it, and in this case that was Chevron. So, it was a Chevron hospital. It was a Chevron school. It was a Chevron facility. But if they were part of the process, and they were key in putting those things in place, it would never happen, they wouldn't destroy their own building that they put there."

Umaru Ribadu of Chevron Nigeria Limited explicitly invokes the partnership model when he describes the new process that Chevron put into place in 2004. Chevron strived to partner with the community in its efforts to reach out to the government, NGOs and civil society. The process was also transparent: Chevron admitted what it could and could not do alone. Where the goals of the community were beyond Chevron's capacity, the company acted as a broker to connect the community to others who could help. The most important principle was, however, ownership. The company handed responsibility for community development back to local people. This was contentious even within Chevron. Deji Haastrup of Chevron Nigeria Limited recalled the internal reservations: "Are you sure that we should be turning over these tons of funds to community people who have never handled this kind of responsibility? We're an oil company. We're used to taking charge of things and doing things that need to be done. We are not used to turning responsibility over to other people."

The negotiations took five months. Professor Ajibola played the role of independent mediator. The professor described that the outcome of the negotiation was an agreement that the community development projects would be determined by a set of committees which involved Chevron, the communities, NGOs and the government. So it was not going to be a situation of Chevron determining that we are going to build a school in this community. It was not a case of Chevron determining that we are going to hire contractor A to build that school. "It was not a question of Chevron determining that, 'This is how much we are going to spend on the school'," Ajibola said. "It was a question of Chevron saying, 'Well, we have $1 million for this set of communities for this year—that is negotiated and agreed to.' Now, the use of the $1 million will be determined mostly by the community, within a committee that also involves Chevron, the state government, the local government, and some development partners, the NGOs."

Leadership by local councils created greater benefits for the community at a fraction of the cost as compared to Chevron's prior initiatives. More importantly, communities that had never had this responsibility for resources rose to the challenge and began to provide for their own goals and aspirations.

The process emphasized the importance of hiring local contractors. This localization enhanced accountability and created a personal connection between the provider of the service and the community, which had been absent before.

In reflecting on the lessons learned, Berry Negerese of the Dodo River Regional Development Council said: "I have come to realize that no one can develop you. You are the only one that can develop yourself." Emmanuel Imeleye of the Egbema-Gbaramatu Communities Development Foundation offers: "If, for the past 40 years that Chevron—oil companies—have been operating in our area, if we have set up a structure like this, today we would not be talking about underdevelopment. Today we would have gone far. Everybody would now be skilled in the development of himself and his community." Emmanuel Azaino, Project Manager at Participatory Partnerships for Community Development believes that, "development progress really is in the progress made by people. It is not in projects. Really, it is the advancement of people from one level of development to the other." Sam Daibo of the Niger Development Partnership Initiative, Chevron believes: "development is not a destination. It's a journey. It's a process. It's not one day it happens and that's it.

It's a process." Professor Ajibola added: "How do we measure real development? I know that the people I met in 2005 have been transformed in many, many ways ... Some of them were people who were just coming out of war—they were raw warriors. Today, these are fine gentlemen who can sit down and negotiate anything with anybody. These are people now who will say it is possible for us to engage any group, any organization in a civilized manner. It does not have to be a violent thing. These are people who are now coming to understand what development is. They are thinking more about how do we really get to change the issues, the problems that we have in our community? ... Now, when there are issues, people are not talking about we are going to destroy the whole thing, they are talking about let us find a resolution. The language has changed."

Deji Haastrup of Chevron Nigeria concludes: "It's right for the people. It's right for the reputation of the company. It's right to improve the business of the company, and it's just the right thing to do for the people in the areas where we operate." God'spower Gbenekama of the Ebgema-Gbaramatu Communities Development Foundation says, "even if Chevron stops their contributions, Chevron stops their donations; we won't allow this process to die. We'll look for a way to get funding from external donors and make this process continue because from now this is just the light. Chevron did well by bringing us together to have that concept. And since we have had this concept, we now know that we can make life better for ourselves than it used to be."

Had AES-Telasi considered these aspects of its relationships with stakeholders in Tbilisi, perhaps it would have placed greater weight earlier on the fairness of the pricing structure. The relative share of its electricity bills vis-à-vis average household income was not sustainable from a societal standpoint. AES also should have relied less on the electricity meters as the basis for its customer relationships and more on trust and partnership. Cutoffs of supply would then have been part of a broader

→

repertoire rather than the first move. Metering at the group- or block-level rather than the individual-level might have tapped into the power of peer pressure. In the aftermath of the Christmas explosion in the generating facility, idle workers might have been devoted to social projects and door-to-door communications rather than cutting off people's power during the holidays.

If you seek to deploy these tools in your organization, be sure to:

- Overcome behavior that undermines social license

    - Avoid coercion, distance yourself from stakeholders who employ it and defend stakeholders against it where possible

    - Go beyond tokenism and tick-box approaches or efforts at providing justifications and explanations alone

- Build the foundation for social license

    - Calculate and present the case for your investment using stakeholders' criteria, not your own, and present that case in a manner that they can absorb

- Enhance interactional trust

    - Increase the number of channels by which your message reaches stakeholders. Make sure as many of these relationships as possible are personal, repeated and deep

    - Consider establishing multi-stakeholder forums moderated by someone trusted by both sides

    - Be aware of, and adhere to, universal norms regarding reciprocity, parity, listening and follow-up

    - Enhance the emotional intelligence of your workforce

- Enhance sociopolitical legitimacy

    - Act as a gracious guest in your stakeholders' homes from day one

→

- Consider how your own network of relationships serves as a prism by which others evaluate you

- Increase the number of interactions between your employees and stakeholders both in terms of the frequency per employee and also by increasing the number of employees involved

- Enhance the degree to which the outcomes of your operational decisions on stakeholders are perceived as fair according to local norms

- Increase the degree to which the process by which you arrived at those outcomes is perceived as fair

- Improve the social intelligence of your workforce

• Enhance institutionalized trust via partnerships

- Help stakeholders reach their own decisions

- Build capacity (i.e., teach people how to fish rather than giving them fish)

Four

Learning:
Humility in adapting to negative feedback in a necessarily imperfect strategy

D AD is dead, or at least he is dying.
   Large projects used to be managed according to the adage "decide, announce, defend" (DAD). But DAD is being replaced by a more participatory process in which consultation with external stakeholders helps to shape the engineering and financial plans for projects. Under DAD, engineers, financiers, accountants and lawyers would develop a plan based on their understanding of project requirements and tradeoffs. The process was a linear and hierarchical one with the greatest authority and power vested in the design stage. Operational efficiency mattered most. The goal of any stakeholder interaction was to minimize changes to the plan as these added costs. Critics were opponents to be defeated, not partners to be consulted. They would be chided for not appreciating the efforts and expertise that went into a design or for misunderstanding the underlying economics.

Jeroen van der Veer, group managing director of Royal Dutch Shell Group, says that his company abandoned DAD after several much-publicized failures. In one case, Shell had planned to sink its abandoned Brent Spar oil-drilling platform in the North Sea. But an international outcry erupted, which culminated with Greenpeace activists occupying the oilrig for nearly a month.[115]

The company's interactions with the Ogoni tribe in southern Nigeria led to even greater embarrassment—and tragedy. Nine Ogoni activists, including internationally known writer Ken Saro-Wiwa, were hanged by the Nigerian government after opposing Shell's activities in their region. Surviving family members accused the company of helping the government to capture the men. In 2009, Royal Dutch Shell agreed to pay $15.5 million as part of a settlement to end a lawsuit, alleging human rights violations, brought in New York by one of the survivors, though the company admitted no wrongdoing.

In place of DAD, Royal Dutch Shell has shifted to an approach that van der Veer calls DDD—"dialogue, decide and deliver." With DDD, company staffers co-design a project with outside stakeholders, including not only customers but also communities, suppliers, governments and NGOs. Undergirding this approach is recognition that project delays and cost overruns were driven by what was omitted from DAD. Engineers and financiers underestimated delays and costs associated with stakeholder conflict. This recognition creates a willingness to look outside for solutions to a project's political and social problems. Where something can be redesigned to address those problems, a project becomes not more expensive but more feasible and, potentially, more profitable.

This kind of approach requires Shell, or any company that wishes to pursue it, to change internally as well as externally. Hiring the right engagement professionals and paying lip service to consultation is not enough. A company that aims to be an effective corporate diplomat must, like Shell, change the way it approaches projects and organizes its internal operations and outreach. To do this, engagement staffers must be able to combine canny, clear-headed data analysis of political and social realities and *internal* diplomacy. Their approach to *internal* stakeholders must mirror the *personal* approach described for external engagement in the previous chapter. They must build their arguments on good data, understand and plan for the normal dynamics of any big project, and be as savvy about internal engagement as they are about external diplomacy. I describe this process and its three key elements—data, dynamics and internal stakeholder engagement—in more detail below.

The old DAD approach required projecting confidence in a decision arrived at with little stakeholder input and mustering a stout defense of that decision. DDD, in contrast, requires humility, patience and flexibility. It begins with the presumption that the stakeholder community is so complex as to render a plan created without consultation pointless. It accepts that planning will take time and require adaptation. Costs, both in terms of time and money, are compared not to the costs of an old-style campaign but rather to the cost of design *and* the delays, protests and disruptions, which the old approach could engender over a project's lifetime.

Data

Managers need regular, meaningful feedback from stakeholders. The Due Diligence and Integration chapters explain the process for data gathering and analysis. But the data must stay fresh. Depending on the project, the optimal period between full refreshes is one to three years. Interim refreshes will be needed to avoid obsolescence.

Interim data can be gathered from informal consultations, including established grievance procedures, meetings and analysis of social and traditional media. The goal is to take the data and subject it to the same rigorous analysis described in the chapter on Due Diligence.

Each meeting, conversation or media-reported comment by a stakeholder can be compared to that obtained in the initial analysis. The smart response, when someone claims that a stakeholder's opinions have changed, is, "What do the data say?"

Software such as Borealis IMS, SustaiNet's Staketracker, the Stakeholder Circle, Augure's ComSuite, the Praxis Groups' Stakeholder Tracking System, Darzin Stakeholder Management Software, Stakeware, GenSuite, and EnviroLytical's Outreach each can connect stakeholder databases with project timelines and implementation strategies. A well-designed system would link the following elements:

- A stakeholder database containing contact information and characteristics, including information on power, salience, social license and key issues of concern

- A contact register in which issues raised in meetings and other communications with stakeholders are recorded

- Social and traditional media mentions (i.e., cases in which a stakeholder acted on or spoke about the project or another stakeholder in a manner that indicates cooperation or conflict)

- Stakeholder maps showing links between stakeholders

- Issue maps depicting priority issues and highlighting linkages

- Implementation plans, including schedules for meetings and advertising, internal allocations of responsibility for these, and budgets

- A grievances registry and process (see Figure 11 for an example from Anglo American)

Such tools, if properly used, can generate objective indicators of the efficacy of engagement and provide signals of the need for adaptation. Possible metrics include the number of reported stakeholder grievances vs. the number of helpful tips or suggestions; the number of organizations supporting the company; voluntary stakeholder attendance at events associated with the company, and the quantity and sentiment of media mentions.

Another source of readily available metrics is a company's internal cost and revenue information. Among the questions one might pose to dig out this information are the following:

- Are risk management and compliance costs, including those from litigation, rising?

- What about material costs associated with theft or sabotage?

- What do staff turnover and productivity look like?

A final source of data is incident reports on instances of stakeholder conflict (which should trigger automatic investigations and follow-up akin to what would occur after a workplace injury). This presumes that an incident reporting system is, in fact, in place—one should be. Operating without one is like living in an old wooden house without a fire station nearby. Assuming such a system does exist, how many incidents are you seeing? What is the trend?

A more sophisticated approach would subject the text captured in the contact registries, together with those from (social) media, to the same kind of analysis highlighted in the chapter on due diligence, thus generating time-varying indicators of the degree of stakeholder cooperation and conflict. The cost of such natural language parsing services is rapidly falling and its accuracy is increasing. Similar approaches are already being used in marketing and should soon diffuse to corporate diplomacy.

The challenge to successful application of this approach rests on managing the additional reporting demands placed on already stretched managers and staff. One manager at a Peruvian mine who was skeptical of the feasibility of data-gathering quipped that, to fulfill all of the official reporting requirements for her stakeholder consultations, she would have to work 12 hours a day in addition to the 12 she already worked. It is true that frustration can undermine good reporting—the adage of "garbage in, garbage out" still stands. If staffers do not see the value of reporting, or it is too time consuming,

Figure 11 **Grievance mechanism of Anglo American corporations**

Reproduced with permission[116]

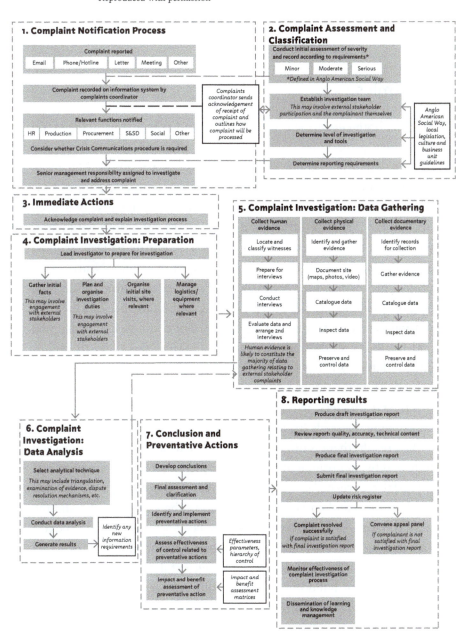

they will not do it well. But if reporting requirements can be streamlined and, more important, the data are clearly used to update strategies and resource allocations, investments in staff time and software are more likely to pay off.

Dynamics

Staffers, both engagement professionals and others, must understand that every project, no matter how well planned, will see ups and downs—often predictable ones. Delivering, as a result, is a far more complex component of the DDD framework than engaging in Dialogue with stakeholders or Deciding upon an initial course of action. Beyond the difficulty of building a Personal relationship with external stakeholders as described in Chapter 3, efforts to Deliver must also take into account these inherent project dynamics. Nearly every project moves from the excitement of conception through the long slog of feasibility studies and permitting and finally back to the celebration that accompanies the beginning of operations. In the planning and feasibility-study stages, corporate diplomacy is often treated as an avoidable cost that is not worthwhile unless a project gets greenlighted. To make things worse, development teams tend to overcommit to stakeholders, making promises that they won't have to meet and sowing the seeds for future conflict.

As a result, there is often an initial spike in stakeholder enthusiasm followed by an upsurge of opposition, eliciting more engagement and a partial recovery. As the project moves into construction, benefits (such as jobs) and costs (such as pollution) become tangible, and the critical nature of corporate diplomacy becomes clear to all. Budgets and staffing then rise, but only in response to the rapid loss in social license caused by construction; nothing catalyzes local resentment like the roar of bulldozers. Another difficult transition arises at the end of construction. Construction jobs end, but the full benefits of the

new plant or mine are not yet being felt in the surrounding community. This is a perilous time. A project is deep in the hole financially,
so upper management is typically unwilling to spend more on engagement. As a result, mistakes can happen, and ill will can fester. Once
operations reach their full scale, resources for corporate diplomacy
are again available, although often only in reaction to bad publicity.
For projects with finite life spans, such as mines, the shift from operations to closure is also fraught with the potential for conflicts.

To some extent, the phases in a project are akin to the phases of
a person's life. Just as you cannot wish away the impetuousness of
youth or the pains of aging, so you cannot prevent natural ebbs and
flows in stakeholder enthusiasm. But you can manage them, just as
curfews can curb youthful excess and stretching can ease the pain
of an aging back. Smart stakeholder engagement is similar. Even the
best plan, well executed, will not placate every opponent or anticipate
every problem. But it will help you in managing them when they arise.

Willy-nilly shifts in strategy can be just as vexing for a project as
normal life-cycle ups and downs. People in all fields tend to overreact
to setbacks, sometimes swapping strategy or staff prematurely. They
are impatient; they want results immediately. Thus, some managers
will start improvising—haphazardly—when they encounter resistance. They will lose focus on their key metrics of engagement because
they fall into any one of several common behavioral traps.[117]

Some of them will obsess over opponents. This distracts energy and
effort from addressing the key concerns of supporters or wafflers.
The personalization of conflict can even empower the opponents by
driving a wedge between the project and its allies: Supporters end
up angry because their concerns have been ignored or because they
feel as if they have been taken for granted. When Alan Hill assumed
the leadership of Gabriel Resources in Romania[118] he was furious
about opposition leader Stephanie Roth's ability to define his company and mine. He wanted not only to set the record straight but also
to set Roth back on her heels. He attacked her and the environmental
movement more generally in a saturation advertising campaign and

funded a documentary that told activists to "Mine Their Own Business." While these attack tactics won him support among viewers of Fox News in the US and others who opposed the environmental movement, it cost him the support of the youth in Romania, who saw the attack-style advertisements as propaganda.

Another potential managerial weakness is an aversion to conflict. Managers afflicted in this way not only avoid opponents but also spend too much time currying favor with strong supporters. They ignore difficult but necessary conversations and decisions that could propel a project forward. Executives who surround themselves with sycophants and avoid addressing challenges are the canonical case of this failing.

A third sort of manager overreacts. This manager feels compelled to respond always and immediately to everything. He ignores longer-term stakeholder strategy. He just reacts, like a spider scurrying toward a shiver at the edge of its web. This undermines efforts to execute a comprehensive plan and engage with a broader class of stakeholders over the medium- to long-term. Managers must resist the temptation to counter every accusation, engage in every debate and mediate every conflict. One could potentially criticize Michael Scholey's omnipresence in Tbilisi on these grounds. While it was important to sway the hearts and minds through a personal appeal, Scholey's many appeals may have confused stakeholders or interfered with the development of a more coherently designed and implemented engagement plan.

Other managers make the opposite mistake. Rather than responding too much or focusing their attention on one class of stakeholders or another, they ignore the need to act altogether. As the opposition makes its moves, this manager is frozen, fearful of the consequences of mistakes. Stakeholders perceive a lack of transparency and, when a trickle of information is leaked or escapes, overreact, assuming this is only a fraction of the truth and a favorably biased fraction at that. A classic case of such behavior is the Japanese government's refusal to disclose full information on the multiple aspects of the Fukushima nuclear plant disaster even years after any risk of triggering a panic had abated.

The most damaging and destructive dynamic is when managers look for internal scapegoats for the inevitable mistakes and setbacks that afflict every project. These managers only hurt themselves, undercutting their ability to respond.

Ideally, managers should engage stakeholders both internal and external to adapt and learn from the feedback that they receive. The intelligence they gather should help them mobilize core allies, sway a sufficient group of waverers and pre-empt opposition.

But even in the best of circumstances, surprises will arise. Unexpected demands will emerge, or unexpected players will force their way into negotiations. Perhaps national legislators have ignored a project but start to involve themselves as an election approaches. The ability to sense emergent issues and respond is critical to the success of a project. Managers must know both when to intervene and when to step back and allow a process to play out of its own accord. They must, in the words of an old American country music song, "know when to hold 'em and when to fold 'em."

At some point, the dynamics may demand change or adaptation in a project. A group of powerful stakeholders may coalesce around a particular demand. Unfortunately, that moment is only the first and, perhaps, the easiest step in realizing such a change. The demand must next pass over the hurdles presented by *internal* stakeholders and the incentives that motivate them to act—or that discourage them from acting.

Internal stakeholder engagement

In an effort to copy the success he had achieved with a similar strategy to reduce injuries and deaths at mine sites, one major mining company CEO publicly committed his firm to reducing stakeholder incidents by a fixed percentage each year. He had an incident reporting system created, and the identity of each stakeholder who participated in protests was determined and logged. Managers' performance bonuses were tied to this determination, much as they had been tied before to targets for production, worker safety or sales. Within a year, the number of incidents involving violence or threats plummeted. Unfortunately, the reason for the fall was not, in fact, a change in the number of incidents but rather a change in the number of *reports*. With bonuses tied to *reported* incidents, staffers had an incentive to underreport. A similar problem can emerge when counts of press mentions are used as proxies for stakeholder support in countries where press coverage is routinely purchased or heavily influenced by advertising spending. Someone who wants positive press just buys lots of ads. These anecdotes highlight that internal monitoring systems are not enough to Deliver on the commitments made to stakeholders after a process of Dialogue and a Decision on how to proceed. Any such delivery system must also account for incentives faced by internal stakeholders—and the unintended consequences that those incentives may generate.

Key elements of such an internal system are humility, patience and flexibility. The historic approach of DAD is, to some extent, the antithesis of this approach as it emphasizes confidence in a decision, which is then zealously defended. The alternative approach begins, by contrast, with the presumption that the stakeholder system is so complex as to render any first design suboptimal. Instead, plans should be developed in consultation with stakeholders, using the tools and processes summarized in the initial chapters of this book. That process will take time and require frequent adaptation. The costs in terms of time and finance of such delay and adaptation need to be compared, not to the costs of the initial design, but rather to the costs of the initial design *and* the negative feedback, protests and disruptions it would engender over its lifetime.

The challenge is not in articulating this vision of adaptation and learning, but in its implementation. Many managerial practices undercut the incentive to adapt to and learn from, over the medium- to long-term, feedback that stakeholders provide through the social license to operate. Performance bonuses, for example, are often based on quarterly targets. Yet it can take more than a quarter or two to cultivate the social license to operate. The best performance targets are often those shaped by consultation with external stakeholders.

Rules of thumb that often drive the allocation of resources for stakeholder engagement can also undermine their efficacy. If a fixed percentage of forecast gross profits or revenue or operational expenditure is allocated for corporate diplomacy initiatives over the life of the project, the inherent fluctuations in needs over the project lifecycle and shifts in circumstances, such as droughts or economic crises, will lead to a disconnect between the efforts to establish trust and the resources available for that effort.

A firm and its leadership must also create a safe environment in which the reporting of failure is accepted, even rewarded. Line workers, low-level employees and middle managers should not fret about retribution. The delay caused by addressing a stakeholder complaint must be measured against the potential long-term lost revenue from *not* dealing with it. There has to be a perception among all workers that corporate diplomacy matters to upper management. While these elements of organizational mindset are the focus of a later chapter, they play an important role in driving the success of learning.

The corporate diplomacy team also must be structured in such a way that learning flows to other key people and departments. Typical corporate silos, where the government affairs, community affairs, and communications operate independently, undercut information sharing. People's tendency is to protect their turf and prerogatives, and this can undercut the effectiveness of a cross-functional activity such as corporate diplomacy. The isolation of such a team can also make them first in line during tough budgetary times because, however productive they may have been, they will be perceived as a money sink.

Typical staffing patterns can undermine collaboration and learning too. Managers in, say, finance or marketing may lack a larger vision of a company's diplomatic goals and the compromises needed to achieve them. They may dismiss diplomatic efforts as too time consuming and costly. To counter this kind of thinking, managers from finance, operations or marketing should do rotations on the engagement team, and these rotations should be seen as critical to their career advancement.

An ideally structured engagement team would combine staffers who rotate through with career corporate diplomats. That way, both types could teach each other, and staffers could share their new knowledge with colleagues once they return to their regular posts. Regrettably, setups like this typically happen only once a firm has experienced a major financial or operational loss due to stakeholder conflict. Then assumptions regarding the importance of external stakeholders and their potential impact on financial and operational performance are more easily revisited and teams are more easily restructured.

Once constituted and empowered, such teams must be able to surmount internal and external hurdles. They must know when to stick to their strategy and alter its framing, communications or positioning. And they must be able to see when the strategy is failing. Their success will depend on the data available, a widespread understanding that consultation with stakeholders may lead to major changes to projects, and the internal flexibility to make those changes.

Diplomats' talking points and checklist

Corporate diplomats seeking to build support for the adoption of this approach and questioned as to the nature of the likely payoff can point to Chevron's onshore liquid natural gas processing facility in Soyo, Angola, as an example of success.

Early on, Chevron identified a list of primary and secondary stakeholders, and conducted over 100 meetings and workshops in Angola to engage them. It hired a consulting firm to complete an environmental, social and health impact assessment for the project to follow World Bank guidelines and Angolan legislative requirements.

Chevron then constructed a number of plans, but, in each case, surprises emerged in stakeholders' responses or demands. After further review, Chevron adapted at each stage of the

→

development of the financial and engineering plan (see Figure 11). It relocated the facility to the opposite side of the Baía de Diogo Cão to address concerns regarding the impact on a sea turtle rookery. It stopped construction for three months per year to address concerns regarding the impact on whale migration. It constructed new housing with free gas lines not only for migrant workers but also for local residents to alleviate concerns of inequity between the two populations. Chevron even hired a herpetologist to relocate snakes displaced during construction, so that the animals would not threaten nearby villages. It developed a plan to protect fishing communities and incorporated local religious customs into its building plan. It also responded to the demands of the local state-owned partner by providing training and capacity building to their employees in the onshoring site in the US. It also conceded to government requests to reallocate offshore licenses to generate more competition among Chinese, Indian and other foreign oil companies, over which Chevron was confident it could eventually triumph. Consultation and adaptation to stakeholder requests has left the project several years behind the original schedule.

Chevron's answer was not always a concession. Stakeholders asked, for example, that the company provide electricity to the area near its facility, but it did not agree, pointing out that that responsibility lay with the country's government. Similarly, fishermen objected to dredging in the bay, and Chevron argued that evidence suggested that the dredging proposed, with appropriate safeguards, was not likely to damage the water quality of the bay and its associated creeks. The company did commit to continuing to survey fish catches to determine whether dredging did cause problems.

As a result of this process, Chevron encountered far less opposition to the project than in similar projects in Nigeria and other similar environments—despite undertaking a $4 billion investment in one of the poorest, most corrupt and conflict-ridden

→

nations in Africa. Just as important, it has strengthened its claim to be the preferred partner of an emerging-market government seeking to develop its oil and gas reserves in a way that benefits both local stakeholders and international shareholders.

Chevron applied some of these insights to its operations in the Niger delta when the previously constituted agreement there came up for renewal. Dennis Flemming explained: "If we recognize that development activities generally have much more success when they have a lot broader stakeholder participation and stakeholder engagement in determining what those projects are going to be and how they are done, those participatory approaches apply to anything involving that process, including the evaluation." The consultation began with focus groups representative of individual stakeholder groups, including youth, women, elders and even militias. The process revealed much greater satisfaction with the project as compared to its predecessors, but also a need to pay more attention to the voices of women.

One of AES-Telasi's strengths was its adaptability and flexibility in the face of negative feedback. Nevertheless, there was still some room for improvement. The data to which it responded was coarse and unsystematic. It should not take near-riots or death threats before you adapt your strategy. The inherent lifecycle of the project was also woefully mismanaged. Expectations were built up too highly from the beginning and inevitable conflict later on was not properly foreseen. There was too much in the way of personalization of the conflict and a tendency to overreact without sufficient time to develop an overall strategy. The strength in this domain came largely from the culture that Michael Scholey created, which embodied entrepreneurialism and mission as well as cross-functional collaboration. More formal systems, however, could have better leveraged his success in this domain.

If you seek to build more of a learning system within your organization, consider the following steps:

- Build real-time or, at least, frequently updated data feeds
  - Grievances
  - Meeting minutes
  - (Social) media
  - Budgetary and financial data linked to stakeholders
- Prepare for inherent dynamics
  - Understand and prepare for shifts over the life-cycle of a project
  - Avoid behavioral traps
    » Obsessing over personalities and personal conflict
    » Kicking the can down the road
    » Overreaction
    » Paralysis
    » Internal scapegoating
  - Exogenous shocks due to shifts in political, economic or social climate
- Develop formal and informal internal incentives that foster true and humble learning
  - Assess long-term vs. short-term incentives
  - Create a safe environment for admitting mistakes and challenging the status quo
  - Build a cross-functional and collaborative structure

Five

Openness:
Strategic communications to reinforce trust and reputation

In corporate diplomacy perceptions matter as much as, maybe more than, the facts. To win hearts and minds, you must communicate not only facts but also images, symbols and stories. People love a good story. Make sure that you shape the story that external stakeholders hear about you. To be sustainable and value creating, however, these efforts must be more than rhetoric or propaganda. They must be linked to tangible actions and behaviors.

Too often, companies stay quiet and let their opponents define them until it is too late. They believe that stakeholders will judge them based on their actions, and that their opponents lack credibility when they make their criticisms. They assume that pre-emptive responses to criticism only invite unwanted publicity and, possibly, legal liability. Most damagingly, they are confident in their ability to respond to any practical problems as they emerge. So they try to stay out of the news, while their opponents are active in social media, blogs and other forums, building a network of allies united around a common vision opposed to a project.

But in our field, as in so many, the best defense is a good offense. At the onset of a project or market entry, stakeholders are still deciding which level of social license to afford to you and can more easily be swayed than after they have made their judgments. The worst time to try to influence them is after a critical comment or attack has been made. Then, whatever your response, the reasonable retorts will be, "Why didn't you explain yourself before?" and "Why should we trust you more than your critics?"

Proactive reputation building

What your company does and has done matters less than what others know you do and have done. Do not assume that your actions and character are known or that others interpret that history in the same way you do. What looks like simple prudence to a business person can seem like exploitation to someone not schooled in the ways of commerce and economics. Recognize that others, including opponents, have agendas that can lead them to define you and your actions in a manner with which you would not agree. And understand that, given the prior misconduct of other companies that may resemble yours in some way—perhaps they came from the same industry or country—an opponent can succeed, *despite the facts*, in portraying you as just another rogue outsider.

Openness begins with the due diligence described in Chapter 2. By asking stakeholders about their aspirations, you develop an understanding of the issues that matter to them, as well as their capability to attain their goals, and the obstacles, even fears, that stand in the way. A good communications strategy begins, not with your story, but with the story of your stakeholders. It puts them front and center. By helping them reach their goals, you demonstrate your trustworthiness and character.

That does not mean neglecting shareholders or internal stakeholders. Companies must meet the opportunity cost of capital and earn a return on that capital commensurate with the risks faced. Non-profits must attract sufficient money and staff to survive. As part of your communication strategy, you should be forthright about your needs and what you can and cannot do on behalf of your stakeholders. If your project cannot survive, you cannot help anyone else.

Stakeholders must understand not only your constraints but also how you ascertain what you can and cannot do on their behalf. Without transparency on this topic, people will doubt you. They will have been lied to before by other companies, government agencies or NGOs. They will have known others who claimed to want to help them but reneged. Their suspicion will not dissipate quickly. By opening up your internal processes, acknowledging your needs and constraints, and explaining how you developed your stakeholder engagement strategy, you can reinforce trust and deepen the relationship with external stakeholders. Without this kind of openness, stakeholders may view you as a checkbook or ATM machine and keep escalating their demands. Openness will help you to move forward into discussion of how you can help each other.

For stakeholders with high power or salience, showing openness is a direct and highly personal process. Meetings will spill over into meals and social connections outside of work. Hotel managers in Bali recount a long list of temple ceremonies which they regularly attend, including annual festivals, weddings and other rites of passage. Participation in each other's ceremonies may further deepen relationships through the development of a common understanding of each party's values. Trust will grow as the barriers between people fall, and common interests will become clear.

Deep relationships require time, and you may have time to develop them with only your most critical stakeholders. With other people, your openness will have to be less personal and direct. You might ask trusted intermediaries to highlight your character and trustworthiness, sharing stories of your work together. Or you might use the media.

The nature of media makes its use as part of corporate diplomacy a delicate task. A media presence can amplify messages that you have delivered personally to government officials and other top stakeholders. But media buys can also look like blitzes—that is, attempts by a rich outsider to drown out dissent.

Thus, care must be used in the development of a media strategy. The full complexity of a project plan cannot be communicated in 30-second radio or TV commercials, or newspaper ads. You must simplify your message and pair it with images and symbols. Tap into local people's beliefs about the world and use spokespersons who have trust and credibility.

Foreign firms are often viewed with suspicion, so strategies that highlight actions work better at winning trust than just making promises. Claiming trustworthiness without showing it courts danger; your words can be perceived or characterized as propaganda. At Gabriel Resources Rosia Montana mine in Romania,[119] CEO Alan Hill sought to shift strategies from a quiet campaign that allowed the opposition to define him and his project to one in which he controlled the message. The resulting onslaught of television and print media was certainly seen by many Romanians. It included a personal introduction from him and his Romanian joint venture partner, featured children asking for a better future for their families, and elderly residents asking why leave the gold in the ground. For some viewers, the campaign worked. But for others it recalled the days of communist dictator Nicolae Ceausescu and his propaganda machine. One local recalled an old proverb—"When you only hear one side of the truth, you know it's a lie."

Similarly, pretty pictures in a press release or annual report of, say, smiling children at a new school, only help if the local stakeholders wanted the school and you were critical to its construction. If you just made a cash donation or built it with little local input, it may be seen by some as more of a bribe or a penance than a contribution to local people's welfare.

Openness in conveying what you have done often will not generate media interest. Presenting the facts through press releases, pamphlets and open-door policies can be useful in addressing stakeholder questions and demonstrating your commitment as well as your openness. But to more broadly disseminate information and shift stakeholder perceptions, more than factsheets are needed. You need local allies.

Allies are external stakeholders who will vouch for you; they serve as your advocates. If they are credible, they will help to overcome barriers to communication and understanding. The choice of advocate is critical. Some strong supporters may be seen as too compromised to convince peers. A good advocate has power or status, but is also viewed as relatively independent or trustworthy. Advocacy from such a person carries much more heft than endorsements from stronger supporters who might be seen as shills. Advocacy by a respected NGO such as Save the Children or Greenpeace, for example, can be invaluable when a company faces allegations of using child labor or causing environmental pollution. Similarly, when Gabriel Resources sought to enhance its credibility with skeptical Romanians in a debate over the development of the Rosia Montana gold mine, it partnered with Leslie Hawke of the local NGO Ovidiu Rom, which is committed to ensuring that all Romanian children attend elementary school. It also enlisted Romanian television personality and film director Dan Chisu. These people were perceived as being independent and having high integrity. Gabriel hoped that their reputations would influence others to support the Rosia Montana gold mine. If paired with facts on the ground rather than rhetoric alone, this could have been an effective communications strategy.

Another approach is to rely on credible outside experts. Such validation can heighten the credibility of your story. It can also overcome low-level concerns that your information lacks credibility. Having an external consultant, academic, scientist or celebrity speak out on your behalf enhances the impact of the message. Another approach is to use allies whose power, salience or reputation enhances the likelihood that their opinions, when broadcast, will sway undecided stakeholders. Of course, people may question whether a spokesperson has just been paid to mouth words. Despite this concern, expert testimony can enhance the impact of communications, particularly if given by someone with a reputation for integrity or, even better, someone who would have been expected to be an opponent.

In these kinds of communications, you cannot rely on facts alone. Good stories matter even more. A report on pollution and fish kills may be ignored, while the same information, presented as a story about the impact of a fish kill on a fisherman and his children, can spur outrage. People have difficulty imagining and responding to abstractions. The ability to see and feel the impact of facts on someone like oneself can transform a fact into an experience, real or imagined. Where that experience links to an aspiration or fear, the emotional response grows. This is why stories regarding lost livelihoods, especially as a result of unfair treatment of powerless people, trigger such strong reactions. At the other extreme, highlighting the attainment of a dream by someone against long odds can have a similarly powerful, though positive, impact.

Linking emotional imagery into subconscious aspirations and fears is a long-standing tactic of the marketing industry. Thus, Philip Morris sold its Marlboro cigarettes, not by bragging about nicotine content, but by showing pictures of a macho cowboy—Marlboro man. And the US Forest Service advertised the dangers of forest fires not by ticking off lives and acreage lost, but by inventing a mascot called Smokey Bear who warned people that "only you can prevent wildfires."

The man who coined the term 'public relations,' Edward Bernays, understood these tactics well.[120] Bernays was the nephew of Sigmund Freud, and he took his uncle's ideas and applied them to the world of diplomacy for corporations and nation states. His first clients in the pre-World War I era were artists striving to build audiences for their shows but lacking budgets to buy traditional ads. He found new ways to create what today we call 'buzz.' He used physicians in New York City to build a word-of-mouth campaign for a play addressing the risk of sexually transmitted diseases. He planted stories in the agricultural or sports sections of mid-western newspapers to build awareness of Italy or Lithuania before an opera singer or symphony from those countries arrived on tour. During World War I, he worked in the Department of State's Office of Propaganda.

After the war, the private sector beckoned again. There, Bernays' first client was American Tobacco, which hired him to increase cigarette smoking by women. Many American men had become addicted to nicotine in the trenches of Europe, where cigarettes were included in Army rations. Women, however, had not gone to war. If they smoked, they did so surreptitiously. Bernays changed that by linking smoking to women's greatest aspiration of the time—suffrage. He planted five women in a suffragette parade down Fifth Avenue in New York City. They pulled their "torches for freedom" from their garter belts in front of a group of photographers Bernays had invited to a particular street corner. Thus, the cigarette became a symbol for women's aspirations for equality. Later, Bernays' clients would include US auto companies, which shifted their ads from fact-based testimonials to emotional appeals about freedom, power and control; Alcoa, which would gain market share for fluoride through expert testimony, funded research and support from the American Dental Association; and Vedanta hair nets and Dixie Cups, which benefited from commercials playing off fears regarding germs transmitted via foodworkers' hair and reused cups. Bernays also designed the duck-and-cover drills as a tactic to spur fear and outrage among American parents that the US government might be powerless to do more than train their children to hide under a desk in the face of a Soviet attack. The campaign fueled concerns regarding the perceived pacifism of Adlai Stevenson and may have contributed to Dwight Eisenhower's landslide presidential victories in 1952 and 1956.

Delving deeper into the case of United Fruit reveals examples of nearly everything one *should not* do in corporate diplomacy. Bernays actually worked simultaneously for United Fruit, which today is Chiquita Brands International, and the US CIA in its effort to overthrow the democratically elected government of Guatemala. The country's president, Jacobo Arbenz, had announced plans to implement a land reform, and United Fruit was one of the largest landowners in the country. Bernays first manufactured a communist plot using a fake news agency he christened the Middle America News Bureau. He then arranged tours for foreign journalists to Guatemala City, where they were regaled by banana-clad female singers and then attacked by pro-communist sympathizers, who supporters of Arbenz and some historians allege were on the payroll of United Fruit and Bernays. (The CIA campaign was led by Howard Hunt, who would later earn infamy as one of the Watergate burglars.) Bernays' tactics in Guatemala were brilliantly effective in the short-term—Arbenz was toppled and exiled in 1954—but, longer term, they were perceived for what they were: propaganda.

Few PR campaigns are as brazen or dishonest as that one. But a risk in any corporate communications is being perceived as patronizing or manipulative. Consider the use of children in ads. Children, in almost any society, embody the future and parents' aspirations; in ad campaigns they inevitably represent hope. Yet minors cannot, in any meaningful way, assent to participate in a media campaign. As a result, their use can trigger a backlash. This is not to argue against the incorporation of children and families in advertising, only to note that it entails risks.

The effort to distill a complex process into a message and choose the right symbols, phrases and spokespersons can easily go astray in this and many other ways. Your message and symbols should be explored with focus groups of external stakeholders and even representatives of the particular stakeholders you are trying to reach. Listen to their reactions of how your message alters their perceptions and why. Assuming their response is favorable and you go with a given media strategy, watch carefully both for the reactions of the stakeholder targets, to ensure a favorable response, and also for unintended reactions. Surprises pop up, and your communications strategy will have to adapt to them. The need for learning does not stop at the design and implementation stages, but extends into openness.

To that end, ongoing analysis and due diligence must track not only actions and expressions of conflict or cooperation but also messaging used by various stakeholders in *their* communications strategy. How are opponents, neutrals and allies presenting their positions? What choices are they making about how to simplify? Which symbols, rhetoric and frames are they using? How effective are their approaches? Does this suggest that you should adapt?

Some corporate diplomats may be tempted to tailor their messages separately to supporters and opponents. That is understandable, but it brings clear, though subtle, risks. Having a single message is simple, and simplicity facilitates understanding. Recall, for example, the straightforwardness of presidential candidate Barack Obama's message of "Change" in 2008 in a country that had grown weary with Middle Eastern wars and was enduring a financial crisis. Despite setbacks along the way, he stayed true to this simple message throughout the campaign. Shifting it or tailoring it for different groups of voters might have enhanced its fit, but that might have also created confusion and mistrust. It might have made him look like just another slippery politician.

Another common mistake is using an inappropriate portfolio of communication channels. Consider again AES's mistakes in Georgia in the late 1990s. Recall that AES had taken over electricity distribution in Tbilisi, Georgia's capital. To modernize the local electricity grid, the company needed to persuade people to pay for power, something they had not had to do under communism. The AES team relied on TV advertising to deliver that message, even though reliable electricity was only available for a few hours per day. AES, in other words, opted for a developed-world solution, overlooking the local context. In some places, with lower penetration of televisions or long average commute times, radio may work better. Likewise, print and billboard ads may reach urban populations but fail in lightly populated rural areas.

Form, too, should vary with audience. The ratio of text to cartoons, symbols and visuals should vary with stakeholder literacy and local norms. Billboards, leaflets and signs may be part of the communication mix, particularly to convey corporate policies and decisions—for example, whom to hire or which initiatives to fund—and the basis on which these decisions were made.

A final question to consider is the extent to which the local media should be considered solely as a channel for communication versus modeled as an independent stakeholder with its own preferences, power and relationships. Where media interests are owned or heavily influenced by powerful stakeholders, it is best to consider them more than mere conduits. The social license afforded by the owner of the media outlet as well as that person's connections should be factored into the analysis of which channel to use. In some cases, it may be preferable to opt for paid advertising over biased or corrupt reporting.

Reactive reputation management and repair[121]

Is your company prepared for an individual critic armed with an iPhone and a YouTube account? Or a decentralized grassroots organization that seemingly pops up overnight, appears to have no single leader, and yet is quite successful in capturing media attention? Imagine if you were the employee at Nestlé who received a call one evening from an old friend warning that Greenpeace was releasing a video the next day attacking the KitKat bar for its association with the deforestation of Borneo and the extinction of the orangutan.[122] How should you respond? Not in the way that Nestlé did! Its initial response included a demand that YouTube withdraw the video due to an infringement on Nestlé's copyright. A low-level staffer also berated critics on Nestlé's Facebook page. Thus Greenpeace's video went viral, ultimately being viewed 1.5 million times and forcing Nestlé to scramble to develop a response that would preserve its reputation as a leader in corporate sustainability.

Crises, large and small, happen even to the best companies. When they do, reputation management operates under enormous time pressure. An accusation of, say, political payoffs might have been made by an opponent that cannot be ignored. Or, worse, something might have happened—maybe a chemical spill or a workplace accident—that portrays your company in the worst possible light.

The same overconfidence that leads to a failure to start a communications campaign can delay a response in a crisis. The risks here, however, are greater. Opponents may take advantage of silence to characterize you in ways that suits their interests. Stakeholders are listening and watching. How will you respond? How should you respond?

Begin by decoding the opponents' message. Who is the target? What is the content and how is it framed? Why? Pay particular attention to emotional frames, no matter how inane those might seem to you. Efforts to portray your organization as a cold-hearted villain motivated solely by profit do not need facts to succeed. The David vs. Goliath myth holds a cross-cultural appeal and makes for a compelling storyline on which the media will likely seize. A good question to ask is not whether an attack has credibility but whether your neighbors would forward a story on such a topic to friends, retweet it or watch a YouTube video about it.

One mining executive told me a story about visiting a potential site in Bulgaria and observing a hunchbacked old woman trudging out of the forest carrying a bull's load of kindling on her back. He imagined her picture as part of an ad campaign decrying his company's forced relocation of a village and therefore advocated abandoning the project. Similarly, just across the border in Romania, opponents of Gabriel Resources' mine in Rosia Montana employed images of gravestones threatened with destruction, an old woman trudging down a road as a giant mining truck rumbled past and a bulldozer seemingly terrorizing a chicken.

When bad news breaks, you may not be able to afford a passive response. Slander sticks. When your organization is an unknown outsider, opponents' words and actions, even when they are little more than innuendo, can dominate. This is especially true when the network of opponents is tighter knit than your network of allies. Managers tend to overestimate the social license afforded to them, and the strength of their stakeholder network, while also underestimating the importance of opposition concerns, particularly those rooted in emotion. The perception that "people will see this attack for what it is" is frequently one based on these biases rather than a thorough analysis of the stakeholder landscape and the risks an attack poses to a project.

Assuming you respond, your inclination may be a denial combined with a provision of key facts. This may appear an effective rebuttal to you and your supporters. But a matter-of-fact approach can seem evasive and cold to opponents and, more important, wavering stakeholders. Responding to accusations of threats to health or livelihoods with scientific data only works if the audience trusts you more than your opponent and, by extension, your evidence and analysis. Typically, the concerns of an NGO on the environment or human rights are afforded much more credibility than those of a multinational. As a result, a fact-based strategy risks reinforcing outrage among stakeholders or feeding the perception that you do not understand their priorities. In that case, your response may lead to the withdrawal of the social license.

What an effective response often requires is empathy, not just facts. If you are afforded a moderate-to-high level of social license, and have a relatively strong network of allies, an expression of empathy is the first step in reframing a controversy. Reframing can take many forms. At its simplest, it can be an admission of failure, but with a twist of humor or additional context. With more planning, reframing can involve an expression of support from a new or existing ally. Here, the endorsement calls into question the attack. In some cases, the ally might even serve as your defender. In the case of BHP's Tintaya mine in southern Peru, mentioned earlier, the efforts to build up trust with external stakeholders through the dialogue table paid off not only in cooperation with those stakeholders but also at a moment of crisis. In 2005, the mine was occupied by left-wing protestors who demanded more benefits for their distant city. The protest was met with a powerful but peaceful countermovement led by local stakeholders who trusted BHP. The government and media descended on the town and heard local residents rally to the defense of BHP. Within a month, the protesters had left, and the mine had returned to operation. An investment in political and social capital had paid dividends in this time of crisis.

An endorsement or defense can carry a lot of weight with skeptics or waverers if it is delivered by a respected NGO or other independent body. The endorser, if independent and credible, can present alternative evidence with which stakeholders should assess the attack. The evidence might take the form of valid alternative measures of your conduct or credibility. An example of the latter comes from the 1994 response of IKEA, the Swedish home-goods company, to accusations of child labor in rug-making.[123] IKEA managed to refocus the debate on the "interests of the child" rather than simply whether children had been employed in rug-making. This shift in criterion was combined with an appeal to an external validator with great credibility—Save the Children, a US NGO. Critics were demanding that IKEA agree to certification guaranteeing that no children worked in its rug-making. IKEA, with Save the Children's endorsement, gained support for a more realistic criterion, which focused not on that absolute standard but on the quality of life of the children.

The likelihood of success with this kind of approach depends on social license. If your company has it, locals are more likely to give you the benefit of the doubt. But if your attacker has greater social license, trying to reframe a debate can prompt accusations of arrogance or disconnection. Where a critic is isolated, however, a shift in the frame of the discourse can prevent a fall in stakeholder support.

At times, it is not enough to deflect an attack. You have to meet it head on, rebutting false accusations or pointing to credibility problems of critics. Rebuttals typically highlight activities undertaken or planned that contradict critics' claims. Efforts at the latter typically combine evidence that the organization under attack has, in fact, addressed the concerns of, or issues raised by, the attacker. The success of counterattacks depends not only on evidence and logic but also on the relative social license afforded to both sides. Stakeholder responses to claims and counterclaims will determine the outcome of a dispute. These responses will be a function of the relative trust afforded to each side. Still, counterattacks, on NGOs especially, can backfire, making you look like a bully; thus they are rare. An exception came in the early 21st century in the back-and-forth over Romania's Rosia Montana gold mine. There, the mine's developer, Gabriel Resources, attempted to push back against environmentalists' objections. CEO Alan Hill funded a documentary, directed by the *Financial Times* correspondent to Romania, Phelim McAleer, and his wife, Ann McElhinney, which accused environmentalists of opposing growth and disliking people. The two have since directed movies attacking Al Gore's *An Inconvenient Truth* (entitled *Not Evil Just Wrong*) and supporting fracking in *FrackNation*. Hill also sought to highlight sources of opposition funding—some of the money came from outside of the country—and the nationality of key opponents, including a Swiss-British activist named Stephanie Roth. While the campaign had the desired impact on the average viewer and voter, the outrage that it spurred among some members of the opposition led to escalation of their efforts to derail the project. The government, sensing an increasingly heated national debate, chose to avoid intervening in the case, leading to the suspension of the mine's development.

After Greenpeace launched its criticism of Nestlé for its use of palm oil in its products, a Nestlé employee inflamed critics by responding with derogatory and condescending remarks leveled against attackers on Nestlé's Facebook page. These included such comments as:

Get it off your chest—we'll pass it on.

Thanks for the lessons in manners. Consider yourself embraced. But it's our page, we set the rules, it was ever thus.

This response, likely by an overwhelmed worker, fueled the fire of outrage and hardened stakeholder opposition to Nestlé's use of palm oil.

The final group of strategies might be called 'strategic surrender.' Here, you embrace your critics' concerns, accept responsibility for mistakes and chart a different course for the future. Once again, the relative social license and structure of ally networks will influence the outcome, even in the face of compelling evidence of changes in conduct. Perceptions of grandstanding or greenwashing are a risk, too. You need to not just say you are changing but show it. Collaboration with critics can help to increase credibility but, of course, is hard to pull off. Stakeholders may be willing to accept contrition, but, if they subsequently feel duped, they may turn from being waverers or lightly committed opponents to outraged enemies. Typically, such an effort begins with behind-the-scenes outreach to prominent critics. It takes time and effort to build trust with such stakeholders. Ideally, a company can call upon the assistance of respected stakeholders who have granted it a high social license. These people can serve as emissaries.

Nestlé's response to the palm oil accusations against it—after the initial stumbles—show how this can happen. There, the Forest Trust, an NGO with whom both Nestlé and Greenpeace had strong prior relationships, stepped in, serving as a referee. Negotiations between the various stakeholders led, within months, to a new strategy to combat deforestation and increase the sustainability of palm oil.

In the absence of a trusted intermediary, a criticized company will have to work quickly to demonstrate a shift in behavior, communicating via supporters as well as mass and social media.

An example of this kind of response comes from the management team that replaced Alan Hill at Gabriel Resources in Romania. The members of the new team, a group of young Romanians who had worked for Western multinationals, recognized that politics, not who was right on the facts, was what was thwarting them. Rather than attacking the opposition, they highlighted the costly actions that their company had undertaken to address the major criticisms. They featured these actions in prominent media ads which appealed to all Romanians, not just the residents of Rosia Montana, an out-of-the-way rural hamlet. Their message: the mine could be part of a better, richer, future for all Romanians and their children.

Diplomats' talking points and checklist

The US military, hardly a fuzzy-cheeked idealist organization, has recently embraced an approach very similar to what is outlined here. A recent report[124] commissioned for the Joint Forces Command by the RAND National Defense Research Institute stresses that the "synchronization of word and deed ... can set the conditions for credibility and help foster positive attitudes among an indigenous population, enabling effective and persuasive communications." As with the employees of multinationals, "virtually every action, message and decision of a [military] force shapes the opinions of an indigenous population: how coalition personnel treat civilians during cordon-and-search operations, the accuracy or inaccuracy of aerial bombardment and the treatment of detainees. Unity of message is key in this regard." Put differently, the US military, after long engagements in Afghanistan and Iraq, understands that it must not just win battles but also hearts and minds.

The parallels between the military and multinationals are striking. The US military is hamstrung by its focus on "inflicting casualties on the enemy," whereas multinationals corporations are hamstrung by their focus on efficiency and profits. Difficulties arise for soldiers and business people due to cultural ignorance aggravated by frequent rotations of key personnel. Other common problems include the difficulty of coordination between headquarters and the frontline, and the lack of training in these

→

areas. Acknowledging these challenges, the US military has sought to shift attention away from a pure guns-and-bombs strategy to one that emphasizes engaging with civilian populations by addressing their fundamental needs, managing expectations, soliciting frequent feedback and responding to it. "It is not enough to do good things for the local populace. You must also broadcast that fact to a wider audience than the direct recipients of your assistance."

A commonly cited example is the strong and enduring positive image of the US in areas where the military assisted with the reconstruction and recovery from the 2005 Pacific tsunami in Indonesia, Thailand and Sri Lanka, as well as the Pakistani earthquake in the same year. These days, whenever the US military begins an operation, one of its goals is to create local champions and positive word-of-mouth accounts of its actions. Instead of bellicose rhetoric and threats, it offers up evidence of good deeds, including efforts to "build schools, dig clean wells and provide medical care," to show affected populations a view of US forces not otherwise offered in local media.

Greater training in communications and foreign cultures, traditions and beliefs is required throughout officers' careers. The training highlights the importance of drawing in the local media due to its credibility. It even includes scenarios of hypothetical adversaries who seek to "fabricate stories and events that paint the United States and its armed forces in a negative light."

The US military, in other words, has come to believe that upfront reputation building matters critically in avoiding and managing the crises and conflicts that are an unavoidable part of its mission. By investing in stakeholder capital, it stems attacks and enables itself to better handle those that do emerge. Put differently, the world's most potent military entity has embraced greater openness to transform itself into a more intelligent and efficient fighting force.

Several key points emerge from this analysis. First, proactive reputation building is of critical importance to avoiding

→

and managing inevitable crises and conflict. Investing in stakeholder capital prevents attacks and lets those that do emerge be addressed through less costly interventions. Second, when crises occur, an analysis of the relative strength of the claim on factual and emotional grounds must be coupled with an assessment of the coalition of support for the attacker as compared to your own network. Depending on the balance across these three dimensions, it may, rarely, be possible to ignore criticism. In other cases, distraction or reframing will be effective in keeping your stakeholders on your message rather than those of your opponent. Direct attacks on stakeholders are risky moves for a powerful multinational due to the potential to highlight asymmetry in resources and tap into or reinforce injustice frames. A direct engagement with the opposition (drawing on the lessons of Chapters 3 and 4), while costly and difficult, is much more frequently required than imagined. Its implementation should address stakeholders' underlying goals and aspirations in a manner that recognizes the power of emotions, symbols and rhetoric, as well as facts, evidence and logic.

Had AES-Telasi adopted a communications strategy that embodied these principles fully, it would have had a strategy that encompassed not only clever satirical television spots (Michael Scholey on television and employees addressing potential mobs in the streets), but it also would have more aggressively and honestly set expectations from the onset and worked to identify customers for whom payment had led to more reliable supply to serve as spokespeople or advocates. It would also have broadened its choice of media beyond television, especially when power outages were rampant. Scholey did a reasonable job earning empathy against the entrenched interests when he was attacked but, again, needed to broaden the media through which this message was conveyed, as well as the scope of stakeholders to whom it was directed.

If you seek to deploy an approach like that used by the US military in your company, be sure to:

- Be proactive in building your reputation
  - Explain who you are, what you can do *and* what you cannot
  - Be open and transparent with stakeholders
  - Be patient
  - Avoid excessive rhetoric and claims
  - Push information on actual accomplishments
  - Encourage your allies to be advocates or even champions
  - Use credible third parties as advocates
  - Tap emotion—especially aspiration and fear
  - Be consistent in message
  - Choose appropriate media
  - Consider whether media outlets are stakeholders too
- Repair and manage your reputation when under attack
  - Decode the opposition's message
  - Respond sooner than you think you need to
  - Go beyond the facts to stir empathy
  - Deploy stakeholder champions
  - Reframe if possible
  - Rebut when necessary but be careful with counterattacks
  - Negotiate via trusted intermediaries when needed

Six

Mindset:
Externally facing long-term organizational culture

So far, this book has mostly looked outward, offering up a better way for corporate diplomats to engage with external shareholders or, in Chapter 4, to develop internal systems to cope with external dynamics. But, as with any organizational change, this approach will not work unless your *internal* stakeholders buy in, especially top executives. It is not enough to have good data and analysis if senior decision-makers do not seize the results and use them to evangelize for change. Even in the presence of this kind of support, lower-level employees must believe too. Change only happens if everyone who is involved commits to doing his or her job differently.

Too often, a company-wide commitment to corporate diplomacy emerges from the analysis of a massive failure that may have even threatened the company itself. Consider the threat posed by the growing ire of youth against Nike in the 1990s for its use of sweatshop labor, which acted as a trigger for the company's adoption of new supply chain policies. The collapse in the reputation of the pharmaceutical industry to a level just above the tobacco sector in terms of its contribution to society helped to trigger a re-evaluation of practices towards drug access in emerging markets. Today, one could surmise that the incipient campaigns against obesity could well be a trigger for Coca-Cola's and Pepsi's efforts on sustainable agriculture and water conservation. Finally, why are so many examples from this book drawn from the mining sector? Look no further than the massive write-offs associated with Rio Tinto's departure from the Bougainville copper mine and the ensuing civil war, which killed 10,000 to 15,000 people out of a population of 100,000; BHP's write-off of the OK Tedi mine; the Uzbekistan government's expropriation of the Muruntau mine in the case of Newmont Gold; the cost of successfully litigating claims against the Batu Hijau and Buyat Bay mines in Indonesia; and, most notable, the bribery scandals and mismanagement of a mercury spill at the Yanacocha mines in Peru.

How did these firms move from these disasters into positions of leadership with regards to corporate diplomacy? In the aftermath of the controversies in Uzbekistan, Peru and Indonesia, 92% of Newmont's shareholders supported a recommendation by the company's board to review the company's policies and practices relating to engagement.[125] The resolution expressed concern that "Newmont projects in developing countries have been undermined by community protests" and noted a "pattern of community resistance to the company's operations." Experts were brought in to interview employees and external stakeholders, and to examine policies and practices. They concluded that Newmont could improve its ability to resolve conflicts and address grievances, and should review and update company-wide standards and programs to guide its sustainability campaigns. The investigation culminated with a report that offered up the following eight lessons:

- **Lesson 1.** Every Newmont operating site should have a comprehensive and integrated strategic management plan for community relations that identifies the objectives and responsibilities of each functional department and takes into account relevant site-specific factors

- **Lesson 2.** Regular and comprehensive social impact and risk assessments must inform cross-functional strategic planning at Newmont's operating sites

- **Lesson 3.** Regional and local managers, in all functional areas, must be accountable for implementation of the company's strategic objectives regarding community relationship building

- **Lesson 4.** Newmont's operating sites must assess stakeholder concerns and engage with external stakeholders in order to understand and effectively respond to their perceptions and concerns

- **Lesson 5.** Newmont's engagements with the community must reflect the company's values and responsibilities, and clearly convey what can be expected from the company in its role as a community stakeholder

- **Lesson 6.** Newmont's operating sites must engage in conflict identification and manage community concerns before open conflict arises, while also respecting the rights of stakeholders to protest against the mine

- **Lesson 7.** Newmont must ensure that its operating sites have accessible and responsive grievance mechanisms

- **Lesson 8.** Management of the environmental impact of mining on water and other natural resources is directly linked to the management of community relations; Newmont must assess and respond to stakeholder concerns regarding both the real and perceived environmental impacts of its operations

The report concluded: "If Newmont is to continue to grow as a company, maintain its production pipeline, and succeed in current and future business operations around the world, it must manage its community relationships more effectively."

The first step for the senior leadership in achieving such an ambitious objective is the articulation of a clear vision or mission statement. Next, senior executives must change the core business systems that influence information flow, resource allocation, promotion and authority. Just as fundamentally, they must create new rites, which highlight the new vision and transmit it to current employees and new recruits. Finally, they must themselves act in a manner consistent with this vision. They must, in the words of Mahatma Gandhi, be the change they wish to see in the world. One particular challenge in this context is the apparent inconsistency between hard-nosed data analysis and humble openness, which are both required in corporate diplomacy. Typically a corporate culture enshrines one set of these values but not both.

Vision or mission statement

An important step in creating a diplomatic mindset is the articulation of a mission statement. That succinct expression of principles becomes a touchstone against which decisions and actions can be judged. Words alone will not create a new mindset, but a clear, codified vision is the foundation for what comes next.

Below are examples of statements from companies in a range of industries. All of these companies have been recognized by various external ratings and perception indexes as living up to their words.

Retail

Whole Foods Market

> We are a mission-driven company that aims to set the standards of excellence for food retailers. We are building a business in which high standards permeate all aspects of our company. Quality is a state of mind at Whole Foods Market. Our motto—Whole Foods, Whole People, Whole Planet—emphasizes that our vision reaches far beyond just

being a food retailer. Our success in fulfilling our vision is measured by customer satisfaction, team member happiness and excellence, return on capital investment, improvement in the state of the environment and local and larger community support. Our ability to instill a clear sense of interdependence among our various stakeholders (the people who are interested and benefit from the success of our company) is contingent upon our efforts to communicate more often, more openly, and more compassionately. Better communication equals better understanding and more trust.[126]

Agriculture and food

Stonyfield Farm

Our mission: We're committed to healthy food, healthy people, a healthy planet and healthy business.

- Healthy food. We will craft and offer the most delicious and nourishing organic yogurts and dairy products.

- Healthy people. We will enhance the health and well-being of our consumers and colleagues.

- Healthy planet. We will help protect and restore the planet and promote the viability of family farms.

- Healthy business. We will prove that healthy profits and a healthy planet are not in conflict and that, in fact, dedication to health and sustainability enhances shareholder value. We believe that business must lead the way to a more sustainable future.[127]

Mars

The Mars Five Principles of Quality, Responsibility, Mutuality, Efficiency and Freedom are the foundation of our culture and our approach to business. They unite us across geographies, languages, cultures and generations. Our Five

Principles are synonymous with Mars and have been guiding Mars Associates throughout most of our company's history. Every day, we do our best to put our principles into action through our work and our relationships with our consumers, customers, business partners, communities and one another.[128]

Hospitality

Four Seasons

The company's guiding principle is the Golden Rule, and as such Four Seasons strives to have a long-lasting, positive influence on the communities where we operate and on the people we employ and serve around the world. We believe that this is integral to our success as a company. This commitment is expressed consistently in our actions.[129]

Kimpton Group

Our mission is to be the best-loved boutique hotel and restaurant company by our employees, guests, owners and communities *and* to genuinely support our co-workers, provide heartfelt care and comfort for our guests and deliver superior financial returns to our investors.[130]

Pharmaceutical

Johnson & Johnson

We believe our first responsibility is to the doctors, nurses and patients, to mothers and fathers and all others who use our products and services. In meeting their needs everything we do must be of high quality. We must constantly strive to reduce our costs in order to maintain reasonable prices. Customers' orders must be serviced promptly and accurately. Our suppliers and distributors must have an opportunity to make a fair profit.

We are responsible to our employees, the men and women who work with us throughout the world. Everyone must be considered as an individual. We must respect their dignity and recognize their merit. They must have a sense of security in their jobs. Compensation must be fair and adequate, and working conditions clean, orderly and safe. We must be mindful of ways to help our employees fulfill their family responsibilities. Employees must feel free to make suggestions and complaints. There must be equal opportunity for employment, development and advancement for those qualified. We must provide competent management, and their actions must be just and ethical.

We are responsible to the communities in which we live and work and to the world community as well. We must be good citizens—support good works and charities and bear our fair share of taxes. We must encourage civic improvements and better health and education. We must maintain in good order the property we are privileged to use, protecting the environment and natural resources.

Our final responsibility is to our stockholders. Business must make a sound profit. We must experiment with new ideas. Research must be carried on, innovative programs developed and mistakes paid for. New equipment must be purchased, new facilities provided and new products launched. Reserves must be created to provide for adverse times. When we operate according to these principles, the stockholders should realize a fair return.[131]

Novo Nordisk

Today, we are thousands of employees across the world with the passion, the skills and the commitment to continue this journey to prevent, treat and ultimately cure diabetes.

- Our ambition is to strengthen our leadership in diabetes.

- Our key contribution is to discover and develop innovative biological medicines and make them accessible to patients throughout the world.

- We aspire to change possibilities in haemophilia and other serious chronic conditions where we can make a difference.

- Growing our business and delivering competitive financial results is what allows us to help patients live better lives, offer an attractive return to our shareholders and contribute to our communities.

- We never compromise on quality and business ethics.

- Our business philosophy is one of balancing financial, social and environmental considerations—we call it 'The Triple Bottom Line'.

- We are open and honest, ambitious and accountable, and treat everyone with respect.

- We offer opportunities for our people to realise their potential.

- Every day, we must make difficult choices, always keeping in mind, what is best for patients, our employees and our shareholders in the long run.

It's the Novo Nordisk Way.[132]

Mining and oil and gas

Anglo American

Our aim is to be the leading global mining company becoming the industry's employer, partner and investment of choice. Sound strategy, a commitment to sustainable development and good governance are essential to achieve this goal. Our top priorities are safety in our operations, and transparency and accountability in our dealings.[133]

Newmont

Vision. We will be the most valued and respected mining company through industry leading performance.

Values

- Act with integrity, trust, and respect

- Reward creativity, a determination to excel, and a commitment to action

- Demonstrate leadership in safety, stewardship of the environment, and social responsibility

- Develop our people in pursuit of excellence

- Insist upon and demonstrate teamwork, as well as honest and transparent communication

- Promote positive change by encouraging innovation and applying agreed-upon practices

Mission. We will build a sustainable mining business that delivers top quartile shareholder returns while leading in safety, environmental stewardship and social responsibility.[134]

Chevron

At the heart of The Chevron Way is our vision ... to be *the* global energy company most admired for its people, partnership and performance. Our vision means we:

- safely provide energy products vital to sustainable economic progress and human development throughout the world;

- are people and an organization with superior capabilities and commitment;

- are the partner of choice;

- earn the admiration of all our stakeholders—investors, customers, host governments, local communities and our employees—not only for the goals we achieve but how we achieve them;

- deliver world-class performance.[135]

Infrastructure services

DPR Construction

> DPR Construction exists to build great things. It's really that simple. We are a company of builders building great projects, great teams, great relationships, and great value. Our purpose and core values are a starting point that help clearly define who we are and what we stand for as a company. They underlie the passion that drives us to be better and different; they allow us the freedoms of our entrepreneurial organization, where people can make a difference with their ideas and hard work. DPR's fundamental, inviolable values and beliefs:
>
> - INTEGRITY. We conduct all business with the highest standards of honesty and fairness; we can be trusted.
>
> - ENJOYMENT. We believe work should be fun and intrinsically satisfying; if we are not enjoying ourselves, we are doing something wrong.
>
> - UNIQUENESS. We must be different from, and more progressive than, all other construction companies; we stand for something.
>
> - EVER FORWARD. We believe in continual self-initiated change, improvement, learning and the advancement of standards for their own sake.[136]

Notice how far these statements stray from the simple goal of profit maximization. Frequently, they identify a company as motivated by non-financial values. They emphasize the importance of suppliers, communities and other stakeholders. Corporate governance terms such as "accountability" and "transparency" appear frequently, but so do such interpersonal values as trust, fairness and even fun. Other elements of corporate diplomacy also appear, including an emphasis on listening, communication and helping stakeholders realize their objectives.

Systems

Employees are not fools. They can see who in your organization wields power and who does not, and which sorts of activities are rewarded and which are not. If you want them to take engagement seriously, you have to show them that upper management takes it seriously. In my 15 years of research and consulting, I have observed no better predictor of weakness in corporate diplomacy than a siloed and isolated specialist team.

The notion that political risk or sustainability can be managed by a small, peripheral, staff is a recipe for failure. Similarly, the idea that key attributes of the social and political environment can be synthesized into a few PowerPoint slides, and that others can use this incomplete information to improve projects, constitutes wishful thinking. In each case, the separation between the core business functions and the corporate diplomacy team leads to the marginalization of the latter. The corporate diplomacy team will then lack the authority and resources to effect real change, and that will gut its ability to attract the best people and give worthwhile advice.

The processes for gathering data and doing due diligence described in the previous chapters are critical to transforming a vision of corporate diplomacy into an operational reality. Values statements will not influence operations unless they are put into practice via metrics and resources. As the old business saying goes, you manage what you can measure. More important than what the leadership team says is what the employees see. Are stakeholder data actually used to determine budgets, strategy or other key operating decisions?

One approach to increase the voice and leverage of corporate diplomacy is to create a parallel authority structure reporting to a country manager or CEO on par with operations. The problem is that voice and leverage are not determined solely by the structure of an organizational chart alone. Creating parallel lines of authority and responsibility for sustainability and other operations in some ways avoids the underlying problem of the need to coordinate. Even if successful, such structures lead to delays in addressing any problems until later, when the stakes are higher. At this point, easy ways to address demands of stakeholders largely lie in the past and a senior manager is often choosing between costly options. A more successful organizational structure involves tighter integration throughout the core elements of the value creation process.

When employees see routine engagement in corporate diplomacy by staffers in finance, operations, marketing and the like, they will internalize its importance. By contrast, when they observe that a company cares about corporate diplomacy only after a crisis, they will internalize the need to keep their work off of the front pages of the newspapers and YouTube.

Similarly, if employees see that promotions or bonuses are given to people who make real engagement part of their jobs, they will infer that they should be doing the same. But if promotions or bonuses are based solely on short-term financial or operational performance, no amount of lip service paid to diplomacy will make a difference. As with any field, people have to be rewarded for desired conduct, and they have to have metrics that link their conduct to diplomatic goals. These could include metrics related to social license to operate, stakeholder cooperation and other elements of due diligence and learning. It is already common to include measures of customer satisfaction, employee safety and compliance in incentive-based compensation schemes. The same logic argues for the expansion of this list to incorporate the social license to operate. Other potential key performance indicators might include a long-term decline in the number of grievances (assuming these numbers are independently verified and audited) and an increase in compliance with explicit policies or standards of corporate diplomacy.

If such metrics exist, the next question is whether supervisors do pay attention to them. Do they draw upon them to highlight strengths and weaknesses in corporate diplomacy in performance evaluations?

Are metrics for corporate diplomatic performance substantive or subjective and perfunctory? Are employees encouraged, or even required, to consider positions in corporate diplomacy as part of a career path to senior leadership? Can they rise to senior positions without this experience? Can they assume key roles in countries in which experience with this expertise is critical?

Let us return to the case of AES, with which I began this book. Recall that AES's goal worldwide was to create a flat organization with minimal bureaucracy. That led to the understaffing of its HR department. As a result, the company had no systematic means of encouraging promising managers to rotate through assignments in emerging markets, such as Georgia. In fact, interviewees reported to me that the best path for advancement traveled through the core markets of the US and UK. AES's values led to an underinvestment in corporate diplomacy that may have contributed to the company's struggles in Georgia.

IBM, in contrast, has tried to integrate corporate diplomacy within managerial career paths as part of the company's effort to become what its chairman and CEO, Sam Palismano, calls a "globally integrated enterprise." Such a company combines an understanding of the local and corporate contexts in a manner that creates value for shareholders *and* stakeholders. It satisfies stakeholder needs and aspirations, and understands how these vary from country to country. It grapples with the inevitable tradeoff between the diversity of exposure provided by short-term project-based assignments and the deeper knowledge offered by medium- to longer-term rotations. It helps relocated staff overcome language barriers and provides them with information on local culture. As a result, its employees develop new perspectives by becoming embedded in the local context rather than in expatriate networks, which may reinforce existing biases.

To this end, IBM creates "global enablement teams" (GETs) of four or five executives from different countries and departments. These teams interact with country managers, serving as sounding boards and sources of expertise. GET members also deepen their international knowledge and diplomatic skills. An IBM internal case study[137] enumerates several benefits of this approach:

> Through coaching and enabling, GET members help CGMs [Country General Managers] pursue several objectives, including:
>
> • Expanding market access
>
> • Deepening relationships with key clients and government entities
>
> • Developing strategies to align IBM and the country's national agenda
>
> • Gaining access to resources and expertise throughout the enterprise
>
> • Enhancing their leadership capabilities, particularly the ability to develop and execute strategy.
>
> At the same time, the country leaders are helping GET members broaden their leadership and cultural adaptability skills ... GETs typically visit their countries once or twice a year supplemented by individual member visits. Between visits, the GETs maintain contact and momentum by working on specific initiatives and forming one-on-one mentoring relationships with country leaders.

An emphasis for IBM is better understanding of government policy objectives and aligning company strategy with those objectives in countries such as Chile, Czech Republic, Malaysia, Philippines, South Africa and Thailand. GET members also strive to build stronger stakeholder relationships with government officials and key members of civil society. Following the Chilean earthquake in February 2010, the local GET called an internal meeting to discuss means to "convert the disaster into an opportunity for political social and economic change." The discussion focused on infrastructure projects to support economic development. IBM provided recommendations for a sustainable water strategy for Antofagasta, the driest place on Earth.

The GET organized subsequent meetings and follow-on work with mining companies. The relationships built through this process have established "IBM as a trusted partner with the new government and set the foundations for future discussions of opportunities across the entire Chilean government."

Half a world away, IBM's GET in South Africa worked with the National Planning Commission to "enable an interactive, online brainstorming event to exchange opinions and gather insights [from] 10,400 participants spanning each of the country's 52 municipal areas. ... The relationships forged with the Department of Planning, Monitoring and Evaluation are expected to lead to business growth for IBM as the country moves to realize its updated national vision."

Another key set of processes touched on only in passing earlier involves recruiting and training. Through hiring and training, new employees first encounter a company's unwritten rules and corporate culture. If they notice that everyone in a recruit class shares a set of characteristics or values, they will infer that they have been picked because of these characteristics and that these represent the company's real values. If corporate diplomacy matters, then the new hires should include some specialists in the area, as well as candidates with international experience, even if engagement per se is not their specialty. Examples of the former might include new hires from, say, lobbying or communications firms or non-profits, while the latter might include engineers or accountants who have worked elsewhere in successful engagement efforts. Without a concerted effort to find and hire these sorts of people, employees may rightly conclude that a company's commitment to corporate diplomacy is just empty talk to which they need pay only lip service.

Rites[138]

Training manuals and training sessions may seem ho-hum, but these, too, send signals about what a company cares about. People will notice if training is allocated to worker safety, innovation, sexual harassment, productivity and employee benefits, but not to corporate diplomacy. The development of codes of conduct and training materials should therefore be seen not only as symbolic but also as a critical signal sent to new hires regarding the importance of corporate diplomacy.

Another important class of rites involves how an enterprise responds to obvious failings. Most companies at the frontier of corporate diplomacy have learned through failure, even crisis. Senior leaders used adversity to their advantage, addressing a problem that may have cost billions of dollars or dozens of lives, and reorienting their organization and its values to pay greater attention to external stakeholders. An example of such a transformation is Rio Tinto's response to the aforementioned loss of the Bougainville mine in Papua New Guinea, as recounted on its corporate website.[139]

> The island of Bougainville wanted to secede from Papua New Guinea. In the conflict, mine facilities and employees came under attack, eventually leading to the closure of operations.
>
> The situation appeared to stem from dissatisfaction of some villagers with the share of the income they received from the mining operation, and with the distribution of this among various claimants. The problems were part of a wider issue about how the income from mining operations in Papua New Guinea should be distributed. Several attempts to settle the dispute were made by the government and the company before the eventual closure, but without success.
>
> Determined not to be faced with this situation again, Rio Tinto committed to building a strong focus on local community needs and issues. Stakeholder engagement entered the corporate DNA.

Less forward-looking companies might interpret events like these as random or unforeseeable, and ignore how their shortcomings might have contributed. When a diplomatic crisis arises within your organization, how do people respond? Is there a post mortem that addresses the shortcomings of your corporate diplomacy? Were responsible managers replaced or sanctioned? Were any internal critics of the mistaken decisions acknowledged and given greater voice and authority?

A less fraught, but still important, corporate rite is the acknowledgment of accomplishments. From newsletters and internal awards to annual reports and social media mentions, many organizations recognize employees for good work. These rites highlight desired values or practices and, ideally, contribute to the diffusion of those values. Are corporate diplomatic efforts recognized too?

A problem in any workplace is the deluge of emails and newsletters that employees receive—and often ignore. Even awards can fail to stand out. Thus, to capture attention, recognition of diplomatic efforts may need to be distinct. For example, at Rio Tinto, a way to highlight the importance of safety after the death of ten rescuers in the Taussig mine in Austria was the introduction of "safety shares" at the start of every meeting.[140] In a safety share, employees describe safety-related challenges they have observed, and the group then discusses how best to address these. If the concern is significant, the meeting can be delayed until the safety problem is resolved. This process highlights the need for continuous improvement in safety practices. It also provides an opportunity for employees with an eye for risks to be acknowledged, and signals to every employee and stakeholder in attendance that Rio Tinto prizes safety. How many organizations have "diplomacy shares"?

Another class of corporate rites focuses on skill renewal. These often take the form of workshops or seminars on skills or topics that can help to advance employees' career. The menu of course options is another way in which companies send signals to employees about corporate culture and values. Some companies in the mining and oil-and-gas industries have made substantial investments in programs focused on elements of corporate diplomacy. Most notably, in the mid 1990s, reeling from the Brent Spar debacle in the North Sea and allegations of complicity in human rights abuses in Nigeria, Royal Dutch Shell created a new engagement training program. It funded the development of an online simulation called Pactio, which focused on the stakeholder-related challenges associated with the development of a Latin American mine.[141] Fifteen years later, Rio Tinto has similarly invested in the development of a stakeholder engagement academy.[142] This four-day training-and-development program "will support us in maintaining and enhancing our license to operate and in turn will support future growth," says Judy Brown, chief adviser for stakeholder engagement." The program strives "to strengthen [engagement] capability as a source of competitive advantage, develop front-line and project managers and build future leaders who are capable in the area of stakeholder engagement," according to Rio Tinto's website. Employees who participate in the program "learn competencies such as the strategic role of stakeholder engagement, understanding stakeholders, building relationships and negotiating sustainable agreements."

About 30 managers enroll in a given Rio Tinto offering, and the company provides eight to ten such offerings a year at various sites around the world. Its aim is to train about 1,000 managers within four years. The University of Pennsylvania's Wharton School's open enrollment program on corporate diplomacy[143] is the first offering from a top-tier business school on these topics.

A final set of rites—celebrations—may seem symbolic but can play as critical role as activities that seem more substantive. Holiday parties or summer picnics serve to unite people and foster a sense of group identity. They also represent an excellent opportunity to engage with external stakeholders who can be invited too. Holiday gatherings and fundraising dinners are not just opportunities to socialize. They can be concrete manifestations of an expression of common interests and a desire to learn more about the values of external stakeholders.

Leadership

It seems an obvious, even trite, statement, but employees listen to their bosses. They hear the way in which executives and managers speak about external stakeholders and observe—and imitate—the ways they interact with them. If you are a leader, what signals are you sending to subordinates? Do you focus on operational efficiency and cost-cutting or do you highlight the importance of external stakeholders to financial and operational performance. Do you draw attention to the need to make investments in stakeholder capital and develop relationships that enhance corporate reputation and, ultimately, success? The stories that leaders share in meetings or at social events underscore the values on which subordinates are expected to act. Privately denigrating external stakeholders, or dismissing their concerns, undermines efforts to shift mindsets. The prioritization of meetings or actions or budgets, particularly when time or resources are constrained, also sends a powerful implicit message. In an effort to win the hearts and minds of external as well as internal stakeholders, what one says is frequently overshadowed by what one does.

Engaging the analytic and behavioral elements

The corporate diplomacy framework (see Fig. 1 on p. xv) includes two elements driven by data and analytics (Due Diligence and Integration), two elements that address effective interaction with external stakeholders (Personal and Openness), and two elements that emphasize internal attributes (Learning and Mindset). Put differently, four elements are primarily behavioral, while two are technical. An important consideration in the development of a diplomatic mindset is striking a balance between these seemingly opposing perspectives. A purely analytical focus may seem attractive to firms dominated by engineers or other data-driven professionals such as financiers and accountants. But hard-edged analysis without politesse can alienate stakeholders; people do not want to be perceived as mere data points. By contrast, emphasizing personal interaction may appeal to engagement professionals, but can lead to corporate diplomacy's continued isolation within the corporate hierarchy. Many attempts to introduce new approaches to corporate diplomacy have foundered because proponents emphasized one side of this equation more than the other. Both of them matter. You must have head and heart, data and diplomacy.

Henry Mintzberg addresses management more broadly in his book *Managers Not MBAs*, but his point about balance applies to corporate diplomacy, too:

> Management is a practice that has to blend a good deal of craft (experience) with a certain amount of art (insight) and some science (analysis). An education that overemphasizes the science encourages a style of managing I call "calculating" or, if the graduates believe themselves to be artists, as increasing numbers now do, a related style I call "heroic." Enough of them, enough of that. We don't need heroes in positions of influence any more than technocrats. We need balanced, dedicated people who practice a style of managing that can be called "engaging."[144]

Mintzberg uses the metaphor of engaged managers as weavers of these distinctive threads.

> You analyze, then you act. But that does not work as expected, so you reflect. You act some more, then you find yourself blocked, realizing that you cannot do it alone. You have to collaborate. But to do that, you have to get into the world of others. Then more analysis follows, to articulate the new insights. Now you act again—and so it goes, as the cloth of your effort forms.[145]

Corporate diplomats also need to weave together experience, insight and analysis. They begin by analyzing the stakeholder landscape and integrating that information into core corporate strategy. Implementation then requires cooperation with external stakeholders, commitment among internal stakeholders and effective communications with everyone. When surprises arise, smart diplomats update their analyses and revise their engagement plans.

A successful mindset does not enshrine one of these elements over the others, but highlights their interdependence in the service of broader corporate goals. It focuses as much on the links and feedback as the individual components. It emphasizes the connection between analytics and conduct, and highlights that success depends on both. A diplomatic mindset neither hallows the external stakeholder's point of view nor insists on trying to change it. Rather, it strives to learn, experiment, evaluate and revise. A senior manager well-versed in corporate diplomacy shuttles back and forth between external and internal stakeholders, learning from both and helping them understand each other. Ideally, both sides will come to appreciate that they still have much to learn about each other and, even more important, that they can better serve everyone's interests by learning, planning and doing together.

Diplomats' talking points and checklist

No exemplar company comes close to matching the customer orientation of the Four Seasons or Kimpton Group nor the patient orientation of Johnson & Johnson or Novo Nordisk. Achieving this level of mindset remains an aspirational goal at this point in the life-cycle of corporate diplomacy.

Interestingly, AES-Telasi had a powerful mindset that placed mission on par with profits.[146] The company's mission was "to help serve the world's need for electricity," which it pledged to do by following "four major shared principles: to act with integrity, to be fair, to have fun, and to be socially responsible." Missionary zeal pervaded the organization, but it did not translate into prudent strategies for engagement.

If you seek to change the mindset of your company, be sure to:

- Provide a clear succinct statement of mission that highlights the goals of the organizational transformation

- Support behavior consistent with this mission through formal incentives

→

- Distribute rather than silo or focus responsibility
- Measures used for
  - » Resource allocation
  - » Promotion
  - » Performance reviews
  - » Compensation
- Human and social capital system
  - » Training
  - » Recruiting
- Support behavior consistent with this mission statement through informal norms and rites. Consider signals sent by rites that
  - Respond to stakeholder crises
  - Mark accomplishments
  - Focus attention and discussion on practices
  - Renew or update skills
  - Integrate employees (and stakeholders)
- Leaders lead by example of their own behavior and speech
- Decrease seeming barrier between analytic and behavioral mindsets

Conclusion:
12 traps to avoid

It would be heartening to provide a contrasting example to that of AES-Telasi to close this book: A firm that has implemented all six elements of the corporate diplomacy framework and earned sustainable superior returns as a result. My students and clients ask me for the example that shows that implementing this framework is possible and profitable. I have to reply that, while I have seen companies implement best practices in each of the elements of corporate diplomacy, I have never seen one company put all of them together. As I have watched companies try to build on success in one domain or another, I have, however, identified 12 common traps in the development of that level of capability. I hope that highlighting these traps, and showing the difficulties of surmounting them, may prove useful in moving companies closer to a hypothetical—but hopefully soon realized—frontier of corporate diplomacy.

1. We don't do that. We're not political. We focus on our business

The first trap is complacency. It is more common than you might think. As recently as 2000, even Shell was complacent. It did not anticipate changes in its external political and social environment. It just reacted. Starting in 2008, the company acknowledged that not only are its market capitalization and strategy influenced by political and social developments, but also that it has a strong interest and ability in influencing those developments

How could Shell have persisted for so long in the illusion that it was not a political company? It had always identified itself as an engineering enterprise: A collection of individuals that overcame difficult geological and technical challenges to deliver energy to global consumers. Even today, the company's website identifies it as a company that "use[s] advanced technologies and take[s] an innovative approach to help build a sustainable energy future." When top managers prize engineering above all else, diplomacy is often sidelined, either because it is seen as a distraction or a waste of money. As a result, engagement professionals are afforded little voice or authority. And their team is severely understaffed and under resourced.

To see how widespread this attitude is, consider the question of what per cent of time most managers would like to spend on corporate diplomacy. I have asked this question of my MBA students and hundreds of executives over the last 15 years. There is invariably a group of participants who emphatically answer "Zero"! The rest accept, grudgingly, that they may need to devote 10–20% of their time to diplomacy, especially as they advance their careers. When asked, "Why zero?" those respondents grouse that engagement does not create value. What is more, there are typically a limited number of seats around the boardroom table. Ambitious business people typically see themselves as engineers, managers, innovators or marketers, but seldom as lobbyists or diplomats.

Changing attitudes requires more than the argument that govern-ments—as regulators, as customers, even as opponents—are signifi-cant stakeholders in nearly every industry. What must happen, instead, is that senior leadership commits itself to reshaping the organizational mindset. Unfortunately, as noted in Chapter 6, such efforts are most common after failures that led to large capital write-offs.

2. Learning the wrong lessons from failure (or success)

A second common trap is to respond to a failure of corporate diplo-macy by concluding that modeling political and social systems is pointless. A denied permit, an electoral surprise or a double-crossing former ally, can sting—and cost plenty of money. But the tendency of both skeptics and advocates to conclude, from a single failure, that investments in new capacities, personnel and analysis are without merit requires deeper inspection.

A company would not terminate its R&D program because one investment failed. Similarly, it would not fire its sales staff because a major client walked away. The difference is that R&D and sales are well-established functions, recognized as central to business per-formance. Corporate diplomacy remains, in too many companies, an isolated outpost, viewed as a cost center. Shifting to a mindset in which corporate diplomacy is seen as an analogue to R&D or sales takes time, effort and success. Failures will happen along the way, as they do in every corporate endeavor. Where bad luck strikes early, or before efforts have delivered results, the backlash can undermine the ability of the engagement staff to attract the resources, people and credibility necessary for long-term success.

Early success, likewise, can breed bad attitudes. It can create a sense that enough has been done. But, as highlighted in Chapter 4 on

Learning, diplomatic data-gathering and analysis must be adapted in response to the regular feedback from failures and successes. Look beyond the immediate outcome—the permit received or the crisis averted—to the data on stakeholders and issues. Which performed as expected? Which surprises emerged? How much did they influence outcome, if at all? By focusing on the need to regularly tweak the process of corporate diplomacy, a company makes it look more like R&D and sales and the rest of the organization.

3. Reliance on local power brokers/cheerleaders or consultants

An all-too-common shortcut is to sidestep corporate diplomacy by hiring or allying with a well-connected insider. This strategy avoids the need to undertake costly due diligence. But it also shortchanges the remaining five elements of corporate diplomacy, which remain critical to corporate success.

Typically, an insider will make a strategy recommendation couched in his or her deep knowledge of a place and its players. The trouble is that strategy will not be substantiated with data or analysis that can be examined. Even when the recommendation comes with evidence, there are reasons to be suspicious. How does the wise man (or woman) benefit? Who else might he or she be serving?

Even more problematically, you are not building your own relationships but rather relying on those of your local champion. That means that you inherit not just this person's allies but also his enemies. To the extent that your champion is part of a local coalition or clique, you, too, have joined and thus become a rival to its rivals. Depending on the degree of bias in the recommendation provided, you may even unknowingly be assisting the coalition in undermining someone else's position.

4. Greasing the squeaky (even violent) wheel

It is natural to pay attention to the loudest voice, the most persistent and outspoken critic, particularly if that person appears powerful. But consider how other stakeholders might respond to that. If they see that whiners and bullies are rewarded with prioritization of their complaints, they may mimic that behavior. Complaints and grievances will escalate, perhaps even to the point of violence.

Any allocation of resources to stakeholders needs to be considered, not only with reference to whether it addresses pivotal stakeholder concerns (i.e., those most likely to influence stakeholder cooperation), but also to whether it encourages fair dealing in the future. Simply put, rewarding bad behavior courts even worse conduct in the future. Examples include rewarding threats or even violence, abuses of power or status, or the destabilization of previously peaceable relations.

Sometimes, it is easy to identify such behaviors. John Ruggie, former United Nations Special Representative for Business and Human Rights, tells of a case in Peru in which a community leader closed down the only access road to a mine. His reason: "They paid no attention to us when we raised small problems, so we had to create a big one."

Other times, violations may be more subtle. An infamous case in Papua New Guinea at Rio Tinto's Bougainville mine involved compensation for land acquisition. Men received the money, but Bougainville was a matrilineal society. The failure to compensate the rightful owners created resentment and family divisions. The competing claims and escalation of the conflict would trigger a ten-year civil war which killed 10,000 people or 10% of the island's population.

5. Internal divisions on prioritization

Ultimately, corporate diplomacy, like any strategic endeavor, delivers recommendations on what to do and not do. Some stakeholders and issues are favored, and others are passed over. Assumptions must be made, and some of these may be wrong. Internal stakeholders will disagree with decisions, and they may also have their own biases, favoring a particular project regardless of its likelihood of success. They may be influenced by personal relationships, internal political rivalries or the quest for status or power.

A key problem is how these disagreements are managed. Do colleagues acknowledge that the process was a fair one or do they harbor resentment and even try to undermine? Do they try to attack the process, their peers or even the corporate diplomacy more broadly? Sniping and undercutting are too common in many corporate settings. Ironically, overcoming them requires attention to the Personal element highlighted in Chapter 3 but as applied to *internal* as opposed to external stakeholders.

Perhaps the most dangerous divisions are those where corporate diplomacy challenges a well-established practice. For example, the security staff may feel that its use of dogs and ex-militia members carrying sidearms is cost effective and appropriate in a country with a history of corrupt police. Corporate security experts may see risks inherent in openness and closer interactions with the community. Sometimes, corporate diplomats must spend as much time convincing colleagues as they do interacting with outsiders.

6. Arbitrary budgeting rules

Another challenge involves resource allocation. Budgets are tight, and companies want to see returns on their investments. In many firms, people follow rules of thumb for budgeting, especially in dealing with activities that do not provide an obvious financial return. They will often allot a fixed percentage of revenue (often 1%). That is damaging in two regards. First, it bears no correlation with the potential returns from corporate diplomacy investments and, second, it perpetuates the perception that these activities generate no returns.

Perhaps more problematic, a strict adherence to this rule would preclude any anticipatory investment in stakeholder capital. Until a project begins operation, there is no revenue stream from which to allocate funds. As highlighted in the discussion of Learning (Chapter 4) and elsewhere, stakeholder willingness to grant social license to operate is not correlated with revenue streams or capital budgets.

A more appropriate budgeting rule would assess the NPV of engagement. And calculating NPV requires upfront stakeholder investments in Personal relationships, Learning, Openness and Mindset.

7. Perfect is the enemy of the good

Some specialists with expertise in data systems over-engineer corporate diplomacy by trying to build perfect data and reporting systems, capturing every possible piece of information about every stakeholder interaction. While a laudable goal in the abstract, such an effort can undermine progress in corporate diplomacy.

The rollout of such a system can take years and require a big investment in information technology. In the meantime, engagement teams providing the data will still have to do their jobs, flying blind while the perfect machine is being built. Worse still, corporate diplomacy will end up looking like a vacuum that sucks in funds but provides little measurable benefit in return. Needless to say, such a perception can backlash, especially if a new management team arrives.

The focus of data gathering should always be on the rapid delivery of material benefits. The initiative should be well designed but cannot stretch for more than a few quarters. Multi-year pushes involving major information technology investments or external partnerships can continue in the background. But short-term successes are essential, if corporate diplomacy is to prove its worth. Skeptical internal stakeholders will expect more than promises of returns in two or three years from an optimal system. They will need to see short-term benefits. A competent team should be able to execute a stakeholder survey, analyze the financial returns of a number of initiatives, and design and implement new strategies, including a communications strategy and an internal culture-shaping component within six to nine months, or one year at the most.

8. Excessive good intentions

Diplomats can also fall prey to excessive responsiveness. A common complaint among skeptics is that corporate diplomacy is just bribery in disguise—but with the same risks. That is, instead of putting cash in envelopes, you build schools, community centers, parks and clinics. In the end, however, the recipients are never satisfied and keep asking for more. The budget increases, but the social license does not. And if the budget does not increase, the social license withers.

I encountered a classic example of this problem at a hotel in Bali. The general manager there was struggling to build a stronger relationship with the residents of the community around the hotel. One of their major grievances was a lack of garbage collection by the government. The hotel initiated a "walk the block" event for Friday afternoons in which hotel staffers would walk the neighborhood around the hotel collecting and bagging garbage. They then took the trash to a landfill. The change in the neighborhood after the first week was striking. Community members appreciated that the eyesore and health hazard of the garbage had been removed at no cost to them. But a problem emerged the following Friday. Instead of taking ten employees two hours, trash collection took four hours, and the hotel staffers managed, in that time, to clear only half of the block. The amount of garbage seemed larger. The next Friday, it was larger still. The hotel staff quickly deduced that the residents were receiving garbage from their friends and relatives elsewhere on the island and that the hotel was becoming the de facto dump. The general manager ceased the program and convened a meeting of the community at which he explained that he wanted to help but could not run a hotel as an island-wide trash hauler. He offered a new policy. The hotel would commit up to ten workers and transportation to the landfill but only if the community committed an equal number of people and the clean-up work was shared equally. He also involved the residents in a grassroots political campaign to get the relevant political authorities to take responsibility for the garbage clean-up.

The corporate diplomat is a member of an organization that has a goal. He or she seeks to engage with external stakeholders in support of that goal. The goal is not, however, to make everyone happy or be everyone's friend. A company is neither a government nor an NGO. Corporate diplomacy is a mix of tough analysis and gentler interpersonal elements in pursuit of a hard-edged objective. It involves difficult choices. Diplomats can be trusted—they should be trusted—but are rarely loved.

9. Arrogance and a desire for control undermine trust

Arrogance afflicts people in nearly every profession, and corporate diplomats are not immune. Specialists can come to believe that their plan is right, stakeholder feedback be damned, and that their job is implementation, not accommodation or modification. This trap takes various forms from the old DAD approach outlined at the start of Chapter 4 to the paternalism embodied in Rudyard Kipling's phrase "white man's burden." Today, this attitude takes the form of the belief that the professionals know better than the locals what a community needs and what will serve its long-term interests.

Having done deep analysis and developed strong relationships, it is natural for corporate diplomats to seek to expand their role and become, in the phrase of Edward Bernays, "engineers of consent."

Ceding control or trusting external stakeholders seems a risk. Particularly where a company is investing substantial cash or making a big in-kind contribution, should it not take on a leadership role? Is not management of a complex undertaking one of the best contributions it can make to other stakeholders? How could other stakeholders amass the same level of expertise?

No doubt, transferring control and decision rights to organizations with less capacity entails risk. But the single greatest contribution that the corporate diplomat can make is to enable stakeholders to overcome challenges themselves. Long after your project is complete and your company has left, stakeholders or their descendants will remain. How well will they manage their future conflicts? To the extent that corporate diplomats have stakeholders' long-term interests at heart, they should focus on this question rather than the short-term costs and benefits of implementing any given initiative.

Deji Haastrup of Chevron Nigeria notes:

> One must be a little humble in the sense that we work for big multinationals, and we are all well-read. We all believe that we are intellectuals. We all believe that we know quite a great deal of things, and therefore we know what's right for everyone. But we don't.

A classic example of this kind of capacity building comes from the dialogue table at the Tintaya mine in Peru (see pp. 89–91). The mining company's engagement staffers believed that stakeholders lacked the background and skills to engage in negotiations. Given that, the diplomats could push for the best deal possible (or at least the deal that they thought best served everyone's interests), or they could train the stakeholders to secure the deal that represented their interests. The first option was more expedient, but the second was more sustainable. Stakeholders would feel neither manipulated nor coerced violating the principles of "free prior and informed consent" (FPIC). And they would not feel that their interests had been dictated to them by foreigners who they might have distrusted.

10. Propaganda, greenwash and manipulation

A related problem, also bred out of arrogance, is the desire to spin or sell a project, rather than building trust and relationships. For spinners, stakeholders are stooges to be bamboozled with ads and photo ops. Their goal is to identify key influencers and use them to sell a project to other stakeholders. The problem here is that spinners do not believe in true engagement.

In an age of YouTube, Facebook and smartphones, the ability to engage in propaganda and manipulation is increasingly limited. Ed Bernays could rely on his power over mass media and the powerlessness of his competitors and opponents. But today, PR tools and tactics are accessible to all. Multinational corporations operate amid sophisticated networks of activists, politicians and suppliers. It is safer to assume that the spotlight will shine on your misdeeds than to assume that you can selectively present your accomplishments and hide your failings.

11. Islands of excellence surrounded by a sea full of sharks

Interdepartmental rivalries and jealousies afflict every company. Corporate diplomats are especially vulnerable because some colleagues may regard their activities as costly window-dressing. Diplomats can end up ostracized. At the project site, they may eat at different tables from colleagues, and they will rarely socialize with colleagues outside of work.

In situations like this, any failing by corporate diplomats, or a budget crunch, becomes an opportunity to undermine the program. A key determinant of the outcome is the company's commitment to developing a mindset that values diplomacy and engagement. Without that, the sharks will win.

12. Moralism and normative goals that antagonize others and isolate specialists

Personalities and internal politics matter, too. You have to choose the right evangelist for corporate diplomacy. In one recent case, I observed an organization with a high-level commitment to corporate diplomacy unleash a moralistic attack dog on various operational units. He lectured and lambasted colleagues for violations of process and law. He demanded investigations. Needless to say, his outreach was not well received.

While extreme, this example is not unique. Given the typical lack of corporate experience with corporate diplomacy, the status quo may outrage people trained in engagement. When they are finally empowered, they may see an opportunity to right injustices. What these people lose sight of, however, is the need to win over skeptics. Realistically, replacement of these skeptics is unlikely. Instead, they must be persuaded. Change and learning will be slow—sometimes too slow for the morally indignant specialist.

Attacking insiders needlessly antagonizes. To avoid the internal hostility, a diplomat's focus should not be on past failings but on future improvement. Certain violations will demand action, but others can be managed over time or deferred. Specialists should use the same personal approach with the finance, accounting, security and operations teams that they do with community leaders. They should invest time in understanding colleagues and learning the issues that matter most to them.

Dancing free of the traps

The path from the status quo to the forefront of corporate diplomacy is littered with traps. The best way to avoid them is to avoid over-emphasizing a single element of the framework. Instead, try to make methodical, practical progress on each element. They re-enforce each other, with gains in one area leading to gains in others.

In facing the implementation challenge, I have seen companies reach two divergent conclusions best epitomized by two contrasting practitioner quotes I heard one day while conducting interviews in a central European country. The first manager was packing his boxes and preparing to return to his home country, bitter that his efforts had come to nothing. His lament:

> Our parent company and our banks all had the expectation that agreements struck here would stand the test of time given [country X's] self-professed reputation for sticking with its deals ... Our illusion was backed by comfort letters supporting our contracts ... Then we had a bucket of water thrown in our faces ... I don't understand why anyone invests in electricity anymore. Who perpetuates the myth that this model can work?

But his competitor took a different approach—one much more consonant with the spirit of this book:

> [Political risk] has to be actively managed. You can minimize it but never fully eliminate it, even under the best regulatory design. You have to dance with the shadows. You have to go beyond what you see on the surface. A lot of it is relationships, not picking the right people, but rather articulating your views and cultivating ties with people who share your goals.

The goal of this book was to teach you the basic steps learned by firms on the front lines of corporate diplomacy. Given the number of players and the differences in their objectives, these steps will continue to evolve. My hope is that what you have read will encourage you to stay on the playing pitch rather than retreat to the sidelines. Watch your peers and competitors as they engage in the art and science of corporate diplomacy. Build reputations and relationships that further your company's objectives as well as those of your stakeholders. Share what you have learned with those that are watching you, including this author.

Endnotes

Acknowledgments

1 W.J. Henisz and B.A. Zelner, "Power Trip or Power Play: AES-Telasi (A-C)," The Wharton School (2006), University of Pennsylvania, Cases 3-5.

2 R. Boutilier, *Stakeholder Politics: Social Capital, Sustainable Development, and the Corporation* (Stanford, CA: Stanford University Press, 2009); R. Boutilier, *A Stakeholder Approach to Issues Management* (New York: Business Expert Press, 2011).

3 E. Schiffer and D. Waale, *Tracing Power and Influence in Networks: Net-Map as a Tool for Research and Strategic Network Planning* (Washington, DC: International Food Policy Research Institute, 2008), No. 772; E. Schiffer, *The Power Mapping Tool: A Method for the Empirical Research of Power Relations* (Washington, DC: International Food Policy Research Institute, 2007); E. Schiffer and J. Hauck, "Net-Map: Collecting Social Network Data and Facilitating Network Learning Through Participatory Influence Network Mapping," *Field Methods* 22 (3, 2010): 231-49. See also http://netmap.wordpress.com/personal-profile.

4 W. Henisz and T. Gray, "Calculating the Net Present Value of Sustainability at Newmont's Ahafo Gold Mine in Ghana (A)," The Wharton School (2014), University of Pennsylvania, Case 92.

5 B. Willard, *The Sustainability Advantage: Seven Business Case Benefits of a Triple Bottom Line* (Gabriola Island, BC: New Society Publishers, 2002); B. Willard, *The Next Sustainability Wave: Building Boardroom Buy-in* (Gabriola Island, BC: New Society Publishers, 2005); B. Willard, *The Sustainability Champion's Guidebook: How to Transform Your*

Company (Gabriola Island, BC: New Society Publishers, 2009). See also tools available from www.sustainabilityadvantage.com.

6 S.R. Arnstein, "A Ladder Of Citizen Participation," *Journal of the American Planning Association* 35 (4, 1969): 216-24.

7 L. Zandvliet, *Conflict Prevention and Reconstruction: Redefining Corporate Social Risk Mitigation Strategies* (Washington, DC: The World Bank, 2004), Social Development Note No. 1; L. Zandvliet and M.B. Anderson, *Getting it Right: Making Corporate-Community Relations Work* (Sheffield, UK: Greenleaf Publishing, 2009).

8 See summary of all three cases at: www.shiftproject.org/video/corporate-community-dialogue-introduction; www.shiftproject.org/video/putting-ourselves-their-shoes-dialogue-table-tintaya; www.shiftproject.org/video/making-monkey-business-building-company-community-dialogue-philip pines; and www.shiftproject.org/video/only-government-we-see-build ing-company-community-dialogue-nigeria.

9 D. Diermeier, *Reputation Rules: Strategies for Building Your Company's Most Valuable Asset* (New York, NY: McGraw-Hill, 2011).

10 *Ibid.*

11 A. Kelly, *The Elements of Influence: The New Essential System for Managing Competition, Reputation, Brand, and Buzz* (New York: Plume, 2007); A. Kelly, *An Evolution of Influence: The Playmaker System 2.0* (Bethesda, MD: Playmaker Systems LLC, 2012).

12 H.M. Trice and J.M. Beyer, "Studying Organizational Cultures Through Rites and Ceremonials," *Academy of Management Review* 9 (4, 1984): 653-69.

Preface

13 M. Watkins, "The Rise of Corporate Diplomacy (Finally!)," *Harvard Business Review* network blog, 2007 (http://blogs.hbr.org/2007/05/the-rise-of-corporate-diplomac, accessed January 22, 2014).

14 Pew Research Center Survey April 28–May 12, 2009: Q6a-j.

15 See www.edelman.com/insights/intellectual-property/2014-edelman-trust-barometer, accessed January 20,s 2014.

Introduction

16 Quotations not otherwise referenced were taken from field interviews with the author in Tbilisi in October, 2005.

17 S. Wetlaufer, "Organizing for Empowerment," *Harvard Business Review* 77 (1999): 110-126.

18 D. Stern, "SURVEY—GEORGIA—Tbilisi Edges Closer to the West," *Financial Times* November 22, 1999: 1.

19 Georgia ranks among the most corrupt ten countries in the world on Transparency International's Corruption Perception Index.

20 F. Schneider, "The Size and Development of the Shadow Economies of 22 Transition and 21 OECD Economies," *IZA Discussion Paper 514* (2002).

21 *Freedom House Country Report* 1998 (www.freedomhouse.org/report/ freedom-world/1998/georgia, accessed January 20, 2014).

22 S. LeVine, "In Former Soviet Republic of Georgia, Bribes Light the Night," *New York Times* February 7, 1999: 15.

23 J. Lampietti, S.G. Banerjee, and A. Branczik, *Power's Promise* (Washington, DC: World Bank, 2004).

24 Ibid.

25 Reuters, "Georgian Energy Minister's Resignation Accepted," April 13, 1998, accessed via Factiva on November 14, 2005.

26 S. LeVine, "In Former Soviet Republic of Georgia, Bribes Light the Night" *New York Times* February 7, 1999: 15.

27 Ibid.

28 J. Walters, "Privatizing Power in Georgia," presentation to the Energy Forum 2004 conference (http://siteresources.worldbank.org/EXTENER GY2/Resources/4114199-1243609322420/EW04_Georgia.pdf, accessed January 25, 2014).

29 BBC Monitoring, "Georgian President Praises Handover of Border Patrolling to Georgia," December 21, 1998, accessed via Factiva on December 3, 2005.

30 Black Sea Press, "Telasi New Owner—End of Dark Nights in Tbilisi," December 29, 1998, accessed via Factiva on December 3, 2005.

31 A. Jack, "Winter Chill Tests Powers of Tbilisi Grid's New Managers," *Financial Times* December 1, 1999: 3.

32 W. Steavenson, *Stories I Stole* (New York: Grove Press, 2002).

33 Black Sea Press, "State Minister of Georgia Promised to Answer 'AES-Telasi' Within Nearest Days," September 11, 1999, accessed via Factiva on December 3, 2005.

34 Dow Jones International News, "Shevardnadze Tries to Reassure Georgians Over Power Shortage," January 11, 1999, accessed via Factiva on December 3, 2005.

35 Prime News, "AES Telasi to Start Reinstallation of Light Meters In Mid-June," May 10, 1999, accessed via Factiva on December 3, 2005.

36 Black Sea Press, "AES-Telasi Company Celebrates Its First Anniversary," December 23, 1999, accessed via Factiva on December 3, 2005.

37 Black Sea Press, "AES-Telasi Manager Submitted Report on Work Done," March 12, 2001, accessed via Factiva on December 3, 2005.

38 Daily Petroleum Report, "Tbilisi Power Plant to Operate on Locally Produced Gas," November 23, 1999, accessed via Factiva on December 3, 2005.

39 Black Sea Press, "AES Telasi Company Begins Reduction in Number of Employed," May 14, 1999, accessed via Factiva on December 3, 2005; Jack, *Financial Times*.

40 Jack, *Financial Times*.

41 Transcription of Russian Radio broadcast Mayak on June 29, 1999 translated into English by BBC Monitoring, "US Energy Firm Threatens Power Cuts to Make Georgian Debtors Pay," June 29, 1999, accessed via Factiva on December 3, 2005.

42 Black Sea Press, "AES-Telasi Accounts Seized Over Debt for Tax Payments," April 26, 2001, accessed via Factiva on December 3, 2005.

43 Translation of Prime News by BBC Monitoring, "Georgian Antimonopoly Service Urges Consumers Not to Pay New Electricity Rates," September 15, 1999, accessed via Factiva on December 3, 2005.

44 Black Sea Press, "AES Telasi Has No Right to Demand That Georgian Government Switch Off Electricity to Industrial Objects," November 14, 2000, accessed via Factiva on December 3, 2005; Black Sea Press, "The Energy Supply of Ventures-Non-Payers Stopped," November 15, 2000, accessed via Factiva on December 3, 2005.

45 Black Sea Press, "Year Of 2001 Will Be Crucial for AES-Telasi," February 26, 2001, accessed via Factiva on December 3, 2005.

46 T. Golts, "Georgia on the Brink," *Institute for the Study of Conflict, Ideology and Policy* 11 (3, 2001; www.bu.edu/iscip/vol11/goltz.html).

47 Ibid.

48 I. Iribarren and P. Lewis, *Operational Changes at AES-Telasi*, 2003.

49 Ibid.

50 Black Sea Press, "Increase of Energy Tariffs May Be Avoided, Parliamentarian Commission Says," May 22, 2001, accessed via Factiva on December 3, 2005.

51 Prime News, "Hydro Meteorological Station Doesn't Make Weather Forecast for Over a Week Because Electricity Shut Down," July 6, 2001, accessed via Factiva on December 3, 2005.

52 Prime News, "Electricity Supplies Suspended to Kindergarten and Polyclinic of Defence Ministry," August 17, 2001, accessed via Factiva on December 3, 2005.

53 Black Sea Press, "Georgian Government Ready to Take Every Effort to Meet Aes-Telasi Conditions," October 15, 2001, accessed via Factiva on December 3, 2005.

54 Black Sea Press, "NGOs Intend to Organize Actions of Protest Against Increase of Electric Energy Tariff in Tbilisi," October 24, 2001, accessed via Factiva on December 3, 2005.

55 Black Sea Press, "Parliament Criticizing National Regulating Energy Commission's Decision to Increase Electricity Tariff in Tbilisi," October 25, 2001, accessed via Factiva on December 3, 2005.

56 Black Sea Press, "Sakrebulo Objecting to Increase of Electricity Tariff in Tbilisi," November 14, 2001, accessed via Factiva on December 3, 2005.

57 Prime News, "United Professional Unions of Georgia Against Increase of Tariff on Electricity," October 25, 2001, accessed via Factiva on December 3, 2005.

58 Ria Oreanda, "Eduard Shevardnadze—State to Provide Help to Needy Population Due to Increase of Electric Power," October 29, 2001, accessed via Factiva on December 3, 2005.

59 Black Sea Press, "Parliament Criticizing National Regulating Energy Commission's Decision to Increase Electricity Tariff in Tbilisi," October 25, 2001, accessed via Factiva on December 3, 2005.

60 Prime News, "The Tariff For Electricity in Tbilisi Would Not Be Increased From November 1," October 31, 2001, accessed via Factiva on December 3, 2005.

61 Black Sea Press, "Parliamentary Commission Criticizing Decision to Increase Electricity Tariff in Tbilisi," November 15, 2001, accessed via Factiva on December 3, 2005.

62 Black Sea Press, "'AES-Telasi' Stating Chaos in Georgia Energy System and Tbilisi Energy Supply," November 20, 2001, accessed via Factiva on December 3, 2005.

63 Black Sea Press, "Parliament Discussed Lawfulness of Electricity Tariff Increase in Tbilisi," December 7, 2001, accessed via Factiva on December 3, 2005.

64 Black Sea Press, "Georgia-AES-Telasi-Conditions. President Approved 'AES-Telasi' Proposals, Supposed to Help Solve Problems With Tbilisi Energy Supply," November 27, 2001, accessed via Factiva on December 3, 2005.

65 Black Sea Press, "President Met All 'AES-Telasi' Demands," November 29, 2001, accessed via Factiva on December 3, 2005.

66 Black Sea Press, "Negotiations on 2001–2002 Winter Electricity and Gas Supplies Resumed in Moscow," December 6, 2001, accessed via Factiva on December 3, 2005; Black Sea Press, "Units 9 And 10 of AES-Mtkvari American Company Launched," December 10, 2001, accessed via Factiva on December 3, 2005.

67 BBC Monitoring translation of Prime News, "'Tbiltskhalkanali' Facing Electricity Outage," December 12, 2001, accessed via Factiva on December 3, 2005.

68 Ibid.

69 Black Sea Press, "Electric Power Can Be Switched Off to All Objects of Defence, State Security and Interior Ministers By the Reason of Indebtedness," December 14, 2001, accessed via Factiva on December 3, 2005.

70 BBC Monitoring translation of Prime News, "Investigation Into Power Station Explosion Delayed By Collapsed Ceiling," December 23, 2001, accessed via Factiva on December 3, 2005.

71 Black Sea Press, "AES-Telasi Experimenting Elimination of Illegal Electricity Lines in Sololaki, With Locals' Assistance," February 1, 2002, accessed via Factiva on December 3, 2005.

72 Black Sea Press, "Labor Party Versus 'AES-Telasi'," June 14, 2002, accessed via Factiva on December 3, 2005.

73 BBC Monitoring of Prime News, "US-Owned Power Distribution Company Complains at Police Intimidation," September 4, 2002 accessed via Factiva on December 3, 2005.

74 Prime News, "Unknown Criminals Robbed Office of Company 'AES-Telasi' in David Agmashenebeli Avenue," September 5, 2002, accessed via Factiva on December 3, 2005.

75 Prime News, "Interior Ministry of Georgia—'AES-Telasi' Company to Solve Problem on Internal Security Independently," September 10, 2002, accessed via Factiva on December 3, 2005.

76 BBC Monitoring of Georgian TV, "US Power Company to Challenge Georgian Labour Party Over Hostile Ad Campaign," January 23, 2003, accessed via Factiva on December 3, 2005; Black Sea Press, "Consumers Must Pay Their Electricity Billings," January 29, 2003, accessed via Factiva on December 3, 2005.

77 Black Sea Press, "Government of Georgia Has to Subsidize Company Aes-Mtkvari," February 10, 2003, accessed via Factiva on December 3, 2005.

78 Black Sea Press, "Accounts of AES-Telasi Tbilisi Electricity-Distributing Company Seized for Non-Payment of Taxes," January 27, 2003, accessed via Factiva on December 3, 2005.

79 Black Sea Press, "Head of Parliament's Budgetary Office Protests Against Providing Subsidy to 'AES-Telasi'," February 12, 2003, accessed via Factiva on December 3, 2005.

80 Black Sea Press, "AES-Telasi American Company Set to Bring a Suit in London Arbitrage," February 19, 2003, accessed via Factiva on December 3, 2005.

81 Prime News, "Program of Ingurhesi Rehabilitation Financed by the EBRD and Committee of Europe Terminated," March 7, 2003, accessed via Factiva on December 3, 2005.

82 BBC Monitoring of Rustavi-2, "Georgia Seizes US Power Firm's Money," April 1, 2003, accessed via Factiva on December 3, 2005.

83 Black Sea Press, "The Accused of Murder of Manager of AES-Telasi Was Released From Custody Under Written Undertaking Not to Leave the Place," April 2, 2003, accessed via Factiva on December 3, 2005.

Chapter 1

84 E. Schiffer and D. Waale, *Tracing Power and Influence in Networks: Net-Map as a Tool for Research and Strategic Network Planning* (Washington, DC: International Food Policy Research Institute, 2008) No. 772; E. Schiffer, *The Power Mapping Tool: A Method for the Empirical Research of Power Relations* (Washington, DC: International Food Policy Research Institute, 2007); E. Schiffer and J. Hauck, "Net-Map: Collecting Social Network Data and Facilitating Network Learning Through Participatory Influence Network Mapping," *Field Methods* 22 (3, 2010): 231-49; See also http://netmap.wordpress.com/personal-profile.

85 The interview protocol provided here was used in the field in a consulting project for a major mining company in Continental Africa in which Robert Boutilier was a sub-contractor. It draws upon and extends his social license questionnaire which can be found in R.G. Boutilier and I. Thomson, "Modelling and Measuring the Social License to Operate: Fruits of a Dialogue Between Theory and Practice," invited paper presented at seminar The Social Licence to Operate at the Centre for Social Responsibility in Mining, University of Queensland, Brisbane, July 15, 2011 (www.socialicense.com/publications/Modelling%20and%20Measuring%20the%20SLO.pdf, accessed July 27, 2012); L.D. Black, *The Social License to Operate: Your Management Framework for Complex Times* (Oxford, UK: Do Sustainability Publishers, 2013).

86 O. d'Herbemont and B. César (eds.), *Managing Sensitive Projects: A Layered Approach* (New York: Routledge, 1998). Note that we have adapted the original labels of their typology to be less controversial if observed by stakeholders. For example, in the original framework, the group we call "cheer leaders" were labeled "zealots" and the group labeled "disinterested skeptics" were labeled "moaners."

87 R. Murray-Webster and P. Simon, "Making Sense of Stakeholder Mapping," *PM World Today* 8 (11, 2006): 1-5.

88 For references to examples in each of these domains see the more detailed discussion in W.J. Henisz, "Preferences, Structure and Influence: The Engineering of Consent," *Global Strategy Journal* 3 (4, 2013): 338-59.

89 See Chapter 8 of R. Boutilier, *Stakeholder Politics: Social Capital, Sustainable Development, and the Corporation* (Stanford, CA: Stanford University Press, 2009).

90 See the work of Tim Snijders and collaborators at www.stats.ox.ac .uk/~snijders/siena/; or the work of Lite Nartey at http://mooreschool .sc.edu/facultyresearch/faculty.aspx?faculty_id=191.

91 See B.B. De Mesquita, "An Expected Utility-Theory of International Conflict," *American Political Science Review* 74 (4, 1980): 917-31; B.B. De Mesquita, "Risk, Power Distributions, and the Likelihood of War," *International Studies Quarterly* 25 (4, 1981): 541-68; B.B. De Mesquita, "The Costs of War—A Rational-Expectations Approach," *American Political Science Review* 77 (2, 1983): 347-57; B.B. De Mesquita, "Forecasting Policy Decisions—An Expected Utility Approach to Post-Khomeini Iran," *PS: Political Science & Politics* 17 (2, 1984): 226-36; B.B. De Mesquita, "The War Trap Revisited—A Revised Expected Utility Model," *American Political Science Review* 79 (1, 1985): 156-77; B.B. De Mesquita *Predicting Politics* (Columbus, OH: Ohio State University Press, 1992); B.B. De Mesquita and D. Lalman, "Reason and War," *American Political Science Review* 80 (4, 1986): 1113-29; B.B. De Mesquita and D. Lalman, "Modeling War and Peace," *American Political Science Review* 81(1, 1987): 221-30; B.B. De Mesquita and D. Lalman, "Empirical Support for Systemic and Dyadic Explanations of International Conflict," *World Politics* 41 (1, 1988): 1-20; B.B. De Mesquita and A.F.K. Organski, "A Mark in Time Saves Nein," *International Political Science Review* 13 (1, 1992): 81-100.

92 See T. Allas and N. Georgiades, "New Tools for Negotiators," *McKinsey Quarterly* 2 (2001): 86-91.

93 See A. Green, N. Barma, M. Abdollahian, B. Nunberg, and D. Perlman, "At the Frontier of Practical Political Economy," Policy Research Working Paper 5176 (2010): 1-32.

94 Ibid.

95 Ibid.

96 W.J. Henisz, "Preferences, Structure and Influence: The Engineering of Consent," *Global Strategy Journal* 3 (4, 2013): 338-59.

97 S.A. Feder, "Forecasting for Policy Making in the Post-Cold War World," *Annual Review of Political Science* 5 (2002): 111-25.

Chapter 2

98 See G.A. Smith and D. Feldman, *Newmont Community Relationships Review* (Washington, DC: Foley Hoag LLP, 2009; www.beyondthe mine.com/pdf/CRRGlobalSummaryFULL-EnglishFINAL.pdf, accessed December 10, 2013).

99 Economist Intelligence Unit, *Corporate Citizenship: Profiting From Sustainable Business* (London: The Economist, 2008).

100 J. Miller and L. Parker, *Everybody's Business: The Unlikely Story of How Big Business Can Fox the World* (London: Biteback Publishing, 2013)

101 M. Jensen, "Value Maximization, Stakeholder Theory and the Corporate Objective Function," *Business Ethics Quarterly* 12 (2, 2002): 32-42.

102 A similar approach is advocated by T. Bekefi and M.J. Epstein, "Integrating Social and Political Risk into Management Decision-Making" (Mississauga, Ontario and New York: The Society of Management Accountants of Canada and The American Institute of Certified Public Accountants, 2006).

103 Goldman Sachs Group, *230 Projects to Change the World, 2009* (www .borsaitaliana.it/bitApp/view.bit?lang=it&target=StudiDownloadFree& filename=pdf%2F78052.pdf, accessed December 13, 2013).

104 See Accenture, *Achieving Superior Delivery of Capital Projects: Accenture Global Survey of the Metals and Mining Industry*, 2012 (www .accenture.com/SiteCollectionDocuments/PDF/Accenture-Capital-Proj ects-Report-Metals-Mining.pdf, accessed December 10, 2013).

105 W.J. Henisz, S. Dorobantu, and L. Nartey, "Spinning Gold: The Financial and Operational Returns to External Stakeholder Engagement," *Strategic Management Journal* (in press 2014; http://onlinelibrary.wiley .com/doi/10.1002/smj.2180/abstract, accessed December 10, 2013).

106 Accenture, *The UN Global Compact-Accenture CEO Study on Sustainability 2013: Architects of a Better World* (www.accenture.com/ Microsites/ungc-ceo-study/Documents/pdf/13-1739_UNGC%20report_ Final_FSC3.pdf, accessed December 10, 2013).

107 The text that follows draws heavily from W. Henisz and T. Gray, "Calculating the Net Present Value of Sustainability Initiatives at Newmont's Ahafo Mine in Ghana (A)," The Wharton School (2014), University of Pennsylvania, Case 92.

Chapter 3

108 See Boutilier, *Stakeholder Politics* and R. Boutilier, *A Stakeholder Approach to Issues Management* (New York: Business Expert Press, 2011).

109 S.R. Arnstein, "A Ladder of Citizen Participation," *Journal of the American Institute of Planners* 35 (1969): 216-24.

110 See www.equator-principles.com, accessed January 20, 2014.

111 The description of the Tintaya case draws on V.K. Rangan, "Corporate Responsibility & Community Engagement at the Tintaya Copper Mine," Harvard Business School Product 506023-PDF-ENG, as well as the video filmed by the Corporate Social Responsibility Initiative of the Harvard Kennedy School (2006; http://shiftproject.org/video/putting-ourselves-their-shoes-dialogue-table-tintaya, accessed December 10, 2013).

112 See the video case study prepared by the Corporate Social Responsibility Initiative of the Harvard Kennedy School (www.shiftproject.org/video/making-monkey-business-building-company-community-dialogue-philippines, accessed December 10, 2013).

113 Henisz, and Gray "Calculating the Net Present Value of Sustainability Initiatives."

114 See the video case study prepared by the Corporate Social Responsibility Initiative of the Harvard Kennedy School (www.shiftproject.org/video/only-government-we-see-building-company-community-dialogue-nigeria, accessed December 10, 2013).

Chapter 4

115 See Shell Corporation, *Brent Spar Dossier* (2009; www-static.shell.com/content/dam/shell/static/gbr/downloads/e-and-p/brent-spar-dossier.pdf, accessed December 10, 2013).

116 Figure taken from Anglo American, *SEAT Toolbox: Socio-Economic Assessment Toolbox* (2012: 73; www.angloamerican.com/~/media/Files/A/Anglo-American-Plc/development/latest_SEAT%20v3%20Toolbox.pdf, accessed January 25, 2014). For a broader discussion on grievance mechanisms see International Finance Corporation, *A Guide to Designing and Implementing Grievance Mechanisms for Development Projects* (2008; www.cao-ombudsman.org/howwework/advisor/documents/implemgrieveng.pdf, accessed December 10, 2013).

117 The behavioral traps that follow are highly simplified versions of those outlined in D. Diermeier, *Reputation Rules: Strategies for Building Your Company's Most Valuable Asset* (New York: McGraw-Hill, 2011).

118 See W.J. Henisz, S. Dorobantu, and T. Gray, "Rosia Montana: Political and Social Risk Management in the Land of Dracula (A, B & C)," The Wharton School (2009), University of Pennsylvania, Cases 26-28.

Chapter 5

119 Ibid.

120 See L. Tye, *The Father of Spin: Edward L. Bernays and the Birth of Public Relations* (New York: Macmillan, 2002); E. Bernays, *Public Relations* (Norman, OK: University of Oklahoma Press, 1952).

121 This section offers a highly simplified variant of the framework for strategic communication and influence developed in A. Kelly, *The Elements of Influence: The New Essential System for Managing Competition, Reputation, Brand, and Buzz* (New York: Plume, 2007) and A. Kelly, *An Evolution of Influence: The Playmaker System 2.0* (Bethesda, MD: Playmaker Systems LLC, 2012; www.playmakersystems.com/wp-content/uploads/2012/07/SSIS_2.0_Whitepaper_vZf.pdf, accessed January 25, 2014).

122 See summary in J. Falls and E. Deckers, *No Bullshit Social Media* (New York: Pearson, 2012) or A. Chaudhari, "Greenpeace, Nestle and the Palm Oil Controversy: Social Media Driving Change?" IBS Center For Management Research Teaching (2011), Case 911-010-1.

123 See C.A. Bartlett, V. Dessain, and A. Sjoman, "IKEA's Global Sourcing Challenge: Indian Rugs and Child Labor," *Harvard Business School* (2006), Case 9-906-414.

124 RAND (2007) *Enlisting Madison Avenue: The Marketing Approach to Earning Popular Support in Theatres of Operation* (Santa Monica, CA: RAND, 2007).

Chapter 6

125 Henisz, and Gray, "Calculating the Net Present Value of Sustainability Initiatives."

126 www.wholefoodsmarket.com/mission-values/core-values/declaration-interdependence, accessed December 11, 2013.

127 http://asbcouncil.org/node/70, accessed December 11, 2013.

128 www.mars.com/global/about-mars/the-five-principles-of-mars.aspx, accessed December 11, 2013.

129 www.facebook.com/media/set/fbx/?set=a.409004779780.179923.80956 209780&l=37b5daf12e, accessed December 11, 2013.

130 www.kimptoncareers.com/love.html, accessed December 11, 2013.

131 http://2012annualreport.jnj.com/our-credo, accessed December 11, 2013.

132 www.novonordisk.co.uk/documents/article_page/document/about_us_vision.asp, accessed December 11, 2013.

133 www.angloamerican.com/about/approach.aspx, accessed December 11, 2013.

134 www.newmont.com/about/values, accessed December 11, 2013.

135 www.chevron.com/about/chevronway, accessed December 11, 2013.

136 www.dpr.com/company/ideology, accessed December 11, 2013.

137 K. White, and T. Rosamilia, *Developing Global Leadership: How IBM Engages the Workforce of a Globally Integrated Enterprise* (IBM Global Business Services White Paper, 2010; http://public.dhe.ibm.com/common/ssi/ecm/en/gbw03114usen/GBW03114USEN.PDF, accessed December 11, 2013).

138 I build my argument using the typology of rites developed in H.M. Trice, and J.M. Beyer, "Studying Organizational Cultures Through Rites and Ceremonials," *Academy of Management Review* 9 (4, 1984): 653-69.

139 http://m2m.riotinto.com/article/rules-engagement, accessed December 11, 2013.

140 See www.riotinto.com/ourcommitment/safety-and-health-4792.aspx, accessed December 11, 2013.

141 See www.prendo.com/simulations/managing-stakeholders-pactio, accessed December 11, 2013.

142 See http://m2m.riotinto.com/article/rules-engagement, accessed December 11, 2013.

143 See http://executiveeducation.wharton.upenn.edu/for-individuals/all-pro grams/corporate-diplomacy, accessed December 11, 2013.

144 H. Mintzberg, *Managers Not MBAs: A Hard Look at the Soft Practice of Managing and Management Development* (San Francisco, CA: Berrett-Koehler, 2004): ix.

145 J. Gosling and H. Mintzeberg, "Five Minds of a Manager," *Harvard Business Review* (November, 2003): 63.

146 W.J. Henisz and B.A. Zelner, "Power Trip or Power Play: AES-Telasi (A-C)," The Wharton School (2006), University of Pennsylvania, Cases 3-5.

About the author

Witold J. Henisz is the Deloitte & Touche Professor of Management in Honor of Russell E. Palmer, former Managing Director at The Wharton School, The University of Pennsylvania. He received his Ph.D. in Business and Public Policy from the Haas School of Business at University of California, Berkeley and previously received a M.A. in International Relations from the Johns Hopkins School of Advanced International Studies.

His research examines the impact of political hazards on international investment strategy including efforts by multinational corporations to engage in corporate diplomacy to win the hearts and minds of external stakeholders. In a National Science Foundation funded project he showed that markets value stakeholder engagement twice as much as the net present value of the gold ostensibly controlled by 19 publicly traded gold mining companies. He then assessed the contingencies that influence the choice of which stakeholder these firms should reach out to in order to positively influence valuation as well as how to best develop a cooperative relationship with that stakeholder. He draws upon these insights as well as examples from large scale construction management, sustainable tourism, development and military counterinsurgency in his current research. His earlier work analyzed (1) the political and economic determinants of government attempts to redistribute investor returns to the broader polity; (2) the strategic responses by organizations to such pressure; and (3) the determinants of the success of individual organizations in withstanding such pressure. His research has been published in top-ranked journals in international business (*Journal of International Business Studies*), management (*Academy of Management Review, Academy of Management Journal, Administrative Science Quarterly, Organization Science, Strategic Management Journal and Strategic Organization*), international studies (*International Organization and International Studies Quarterly*) and sociology (*American Sociological Review*). This research has been profiled for managers in *Harvard Business Review, Brunswick Review, Accountability.org, Motley Fool, TriplePundit, Investor Relations Web Report, The Public Affairs Council, The Penn Gazette* and *Knowledge@Wharton*. He served as a Departmental Editor at the *Journal of International Business Studies* and now serves as an Associate Editor at *Strategic Management Journal*. He is a Fellow of the Academy of International Business.

Witold has won multiple teaching awards at the undergraduate and graduate levels for his elective courses that highlight the importance of integrating a deep understanding of political and social risk factors into the design of an organization's global strategy. He has authored teaching cases on the experiences of AES Corporation in the Republic of Georgia, the management of the bankruptcy of Thai Petrochemical Industries, the development of the Rosia Montana gold mine in Romania and the financial valuation of sustainability initiatives at Newmont's Ahafo mine in Ghana. He also teaches sessions on Corporate Diplomacy for multiple open enrollment and custom Executive Education programs at the Wharton School including serving as Academic Director for a 3.5 day open enrollment program on the topic.

Witold has served as a consultant for AngloGold Ashanti, Rio Tinto, Shell Corporation, Maritime Financial Group, The World Bank, The Inter-American Development Bank, The Rand Corporation, The Central Intelligence Agency, Computer Sciences Corporation (CSC), Science Applications International Corporation (SAIC), Department of Homeland Security, The Conference Board, Eurasia Group, Hynix Semiconductor, Willkie Farr & Gallagher LLP and Philippine Long Distance Telephone Company (PLDT). He previously worked for the International Monetary Fund. He is currently a principal in the political risk management consultancy PRIMA LLC.

For the latest Corporate Diplomacy tools and news, see www.corporate diplomacy.com; join the Corporate Diplomacy group on LinkedIn; or follow @whenisz on Twitter.

Index

NOTE: Page numbers in *italics* refer to figures.

Index 232